500

things to know about
THE ANCIENT
WORLD

Carolyn Howitt

THE BRITISH MUSEUM PRESS

To Lewis and Ines

© The Trustees of the British Museum 2007

Published by British Museum Press
A division of The British Museum Company Ltd
38 Russell Square, London WC1B 3QQ

ISBN-13: 978-0-7141-3118-4

Carolyn Howitt has asserted her right to be identified as the author of this work

A catalogue record for this title is available from the British Library

Designed by Turchini Design
Printed and bound by C&C, China.

Start here to discover 500 of the most amazing facts about the people, places and things of the past – all collected from the experts at the British Museum. Choose a chapter that interests you, or just open the book and dip in. Have fun!

Contents

Animals	4	Society	92
Death	10	The spiritual world	98
Family life	24	Sport	112
Fashion	36	Towns and buildings	118
Food and drink	46	War	130
Having fun	52	Writing	140
Inventions	60	Find out more	152
Medicine and illness	72		
Rulers	80		

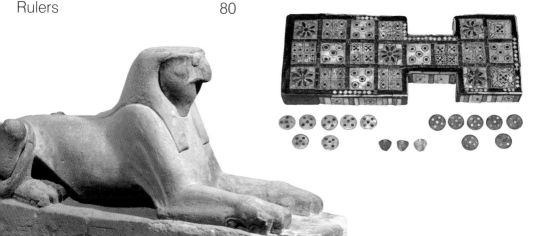

Animals

1   An ancient Egyptian farmer called one of his cows Mehet-weret, 'Great-Flood'. It was crucial for Egyptian farmers that the River Nile should flood well each year and make the soil fertile so that their crops would grow.

2   One Egyptian man from Thebes called his dog En-mereni (which means 'I don't like anybody'!).

TEN FACTS
about cats in ancient Egypt

3   The word for cat in Egyptian was *miu*.

4   Pet cats are often shown in tomb paintings sitting under their owner's chair.

5   Cats were sacred to the goddess Bastet, who is often shown as a woman with a cat's head.

6   The sun-god sometimes appeared in the form of a cat. Egyptian Books of the Dead sometimes show a cat killing the serpent Apophis, the sun-god's enemy.

7   Some mummies contain incomplete cat skeletons, so people who paid for cat mummies to offer to the goddess were ripped off.

8   One writer said that when a cat died, its owners shaved their eyebrows off in mourning.

9   Sacred cats were mummified in thousands and buried in special cemeteries.

10 Seeing a large cat in a dream was lucky, and meant there would be a good harvest.

11 A famous Wisdom Text giving advice on how to live a good life says, 'Do not laugh at a cat'.

12 Egyptians out hunting birds trained their cats to fetch back the birds they had shot down with arrows.

Mummy of a cat from Abydos, Egypt, 1st century AD.

13

Baboons were sometimes trained by the Egyptians to help them pick fruit at harvest time.

Copy of a painting from the tomb of Knumhotep at Beni Hasan.

14

The scarab beetle lays its eggs in a ball of dung, then rolls the ball along. When the young beetles hatch, it looks as if they are coming miraculously out of the dung. Because of this, Egyptians thought the scarab beetle meant rebirth.

Scarab amulet from Egypt.

15

There were no rabbits in ancient Egypt. This hieroglyphic sign shows a hare.

16

Rabbits are not native to Britain. They were introduced by the Normans in AD 1066. However, archaeologists have found the remains of a meal including rabbit bones on a Roman site in eastern England. Did the Romans bring rabbit stew with them when they invaded in AD 43?

17

Early inhabitants of Britain such as Celts and Anglo-Saxons did not have pets in the same way that we do today. All animals had a use, so dogs were kept for hunting and cats for catching mice.

18

There were wolves in Anglo-Saxon England. They were feared because they were dangerous animals, but also admired as being brave and strong.

19

Many ancient Minoan pictures show the dangerous sport of bull-leaping, in which young men and women somersaulted over the horns of a charging bull.

Bronze bull and acrobat from Minoan Crete, about 1700–1450 BC.

20

In ancient China fishermen used cormorants to help them catch fish. Lamps shining from their boats attracted fish to the surface of the water, where the birds swooped down and picked them up. Neck collars stopped the birds eating the fish, which the fishermen then took away from them. This kind of fishing is still found in parts of China today.

21

There were no horses in North America until the Spanish brought them in the sixteenth century AD. The Native Americans weren't allowed to buy any, but they managed to get hold of strays, or steal some. The arrival of the horse completely changed their way of life. Now they could travel long distances, and hunting was much easier.

22

The Native American peoples who lived on the plains of North America depended on buffalo for their living. They used every part of the animal, eating the meat, using the skins for tipi covers and clothes and the bones for tools. There were around fifty million buffalo when the Europeans first arrived. But by the end of the 1880s white settlers had killed nearly all of them. There were fewer than 1000 buffalo left.

Blackfoot buffalo robe from North America, before AD 1868.

6

Strange creatures of legend

SEVEN FACTS
about dragons

23 Dragons are international. Stories about them have been told in many cultures for thousands of years.

24 One of the earliest dragons to be pictured is the *mushhushshu*, or snake-dragon, of Mesopotamia. King Nebuchadnezzar II (604–562 BC) put snake-dragons on the gates of Babylon.

25 Often dragons are frightening or evil, but Chinese dragons are a symbol of good luck.

26 Chinese dragons are usually shown with three or four claws. Only the emperor and his family could wear clothes or use objects decorated with five-clawed dragons.

27 Some ancient European peoples used fierce dragons as figureheads on their ships. Sea journeys were dangerous and the dragons were there to scare away evil forces.

28 The night before St Margaret died (so the story goes) the devil appeared to her in the form of a dragon. It swallowed her, but the cross she was wearing stuck in its throat and it was forced to cough her out.

29 St George was a Roman soldier in Palestine around AD 300. Sadly, he probably never killed a dragon.

Dragon figurehead from a ship, 4th–6th century AD.

A five-clawed dragon on a Chinese enamel jar, Ming dynasty, AD 1426–35.

Icon of St George and the dragon, from Russia, late 14th century AD.

7

FIVE
mixed-up creatures

Many cultures have stories about creatures made up from the body parts of different animals.

30 Griffin: this creature from ancient Greece and Persia had the head and wings of an eagle and the body, feet and claws of a lion. Greek griffins had a spike on their head.

31 The Devourer: an ancient Egyptian monster, part-crocodile, part-lion, part-hippo. The Devourer ate anyone who didn't make it past the judges into the Afterlife.

Lion-griffin ornament from the Oxus treasure, Achaemenid Persian, 5th–4th century BC.

The Devourer. From the Papyrus of Ani, around 1275 BC.

32 Chimaera: the ancient Etruscans and Greeks told stories about these creatures, which could be part-lion, part-goat, part-snake and also have wings.

33 Hippocamp: a Greek sea creature, half horse, half fish, with a serpent's tail.

34 Sphinx: in ancient Egypt, the sphinx had the body of a lion and the head of another creature, often (but not always) human.

Hawk-headed sphinx from Egypt, about 1250 BC.

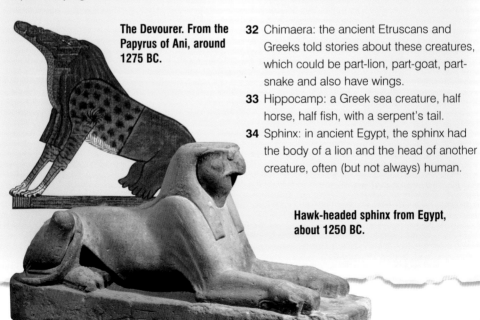

35

Pegasus was the famous winged horse of ancient Greek legend. He sprang from the blood of the monster Medusa when she was slain by Perseus.

36

The Chinese mythical beast called a *qilin* was a kind of unicorn with a horse's hooves, the body of a stag, and a single long horn on its forehead. *Qilins* were thought to announce the birth of a genius child, so pictures of them were often put near cradles for good luck.

38

In legend, the beautiful phoenix bird lays a single egg on to its funeral pyre before it dies. It is then born again from the egg in the flames. In Chinese legend, the phoenix is simply immortal.

Chinese jade phoenix, 10th–11th century AD.

37

When the Mayans of ancient Mexico killed an animal while out hunting, they would say sorry to the god of hunting, and explain exactly why they had done it. The Mayans believed that if they killed more animals than they needed, the gods of hunting would be angry and not let them catch any animals the next time.

Death

After you died in ancient

ROME

39 Romans thought it was lucky to breathe in the last gasp of a dying person. The eldest male Roman family member would be summoned to the bedside to try and inhale it.

40 Dead people were laid out in their houses for a week. They could get very smelly during this time!

41

A dead body was taken to a cemetery. Family members processed alongside wearing masks showing the faces of dead ancestors.

Tomb portraits of a married couple who lived in Rome during the reign of emperor Augustus.

42

The Roman emperor Septimius Severus (reigned AD 193–211) died in York, so a wax effigy was made of his body so that it could go through the funeral rites back in Rome. This waxwork was treated by doctors as if it were dying, then it took part in several ceremonies. Finally it was placed on a huge funeral pyre made up of several wooden levels, rather like a vast wedding cake. As the flames took hold, an eagle was released from the top of the pyre, 'taking the soul of the emperor from earth to heaven'.

Marble statue of the emperor Septimius Severus in military uniform.

43 Romans built funeral pyres out of logs, with the body placed high up on top. The corpse's eyes were left open so the dead person could see the heavens. At one funeral, according to the writer Pliny, the flames were so fierce that the body was thrown off the pyre. The family could not get it to stay on the pyre because the heat was too great.

44 Rich Romans would sometimes pay for professional mourners to join their funeral processions. Their perfect wailing and moaning would add just the right touch to the occasion.

Death in ancient Egypt

EGYPTIAN MUMMIES

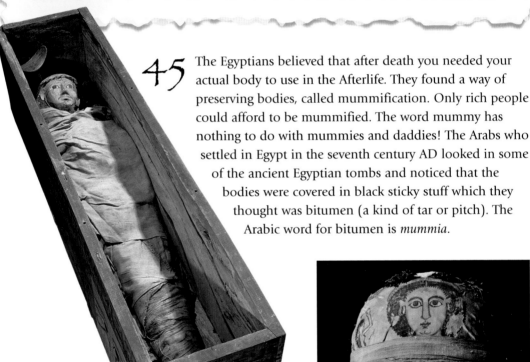

45 The Egyptians believed that after death you needed your actual body to use in the Afterlife. They found a way of preserving bodies, called mummification. Only rich people could afford to be mummified. The word mummy has nothing to do with mummies and daddies! The Arabs who settled in Egypt in the seventh century AD looked in some of the ancient Egyptian tombs and noticed that the bodies were covered in black sticky stuff which they thought was bitumen (a kind of tar or pitch). The Arabic word for bitumen is *mummia*.

The mummy and coffin of Ankhef, an official of the Middle Kingdom period.

Mummy of Cleopatra, a young girl from Thebes, Egypt, 2nd century AD. (This is not the famous queen Cleopatra!)

46 HOW TO MAKE A MUMMY

WARNING
THIS IS DEFINITELY NOT SOMETHING TO TRY AT HOME.

1 Take the brain out in pieces through the nose. Throw it away.

Probe used to remove the brain.

2 Cut a deep slash across the lower left stomach. Through this pull out the liver, lungs, stomach and intestines.

3 Dry these organs out, cover them with natron salt and resin (gum from coniferous trees), wrap them in linen, then put them back into the corpse. (In the early days of mummy-making, you would place the organs into special canopic jars, which were buried with the mummy.)

4 Whatever you do, don't touch the heart. It is the soul of the person.

5 The eyes will shrivel up. Replace them with stone or glass eyes so the person can see in the Afterlife.

6 Cover the body with natron salt and pack more inside. Leave it for about forty days until all moisture is gone.

7 Fill up the empty spaces inside the body with rolls of cloth, spices or sawdust and coat the body with melted resin.

8 Wrap the body in layer after layer of linen strips and sheets. Place in a wooden coffin.

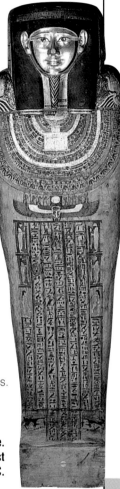

Wooden coffin with a gilded face. It belonged to Hornedjitef, a priest from Thebes. 3rd century BC.

47

The Egyptians sometimes mummified their pets and other animals, as well as their relatives. From about 747 BC many different animals were mummified, including crocodiles, eels, baboons, falcons, jackals and bulls. The Egyptians thought that these animals were representations of the gods on earth.

Mummy of a jackal or dog from Thebes, Egypt, after 30 BC.

Death customs around the world

48 A Viking warrior's body could be placed on his ship when he died and the whole thing set alight with flaming arrows before being cast off to drift on the waves.

49 'Earth laid upon a corpse' is an ancient Scottish funeral custom. The body was buried with a plate of earth and salt on its chest. Earth showed that the body would decay, and salt represented the soul, which would continue on.

50 Jade has always been very valuable in China. People believed that it stopped dead bodies rotting away. At one time jade was used to plug up all the holes in a corpse, and a jade cicada (like a grasshopper) was placed on the tongue.

Lindow Man as he looks today. He died mid-1st century AD.

Jade cicada from China, Han dynasty, 206 BC–AD 220.

51 Lindow Man's body was found in Lindow Moss, a peat bog in Cheshire, northern England. The young man had been killed in what may have been a special ceremony – first he was struck hard on the head (and also in the back), and a thick cord around his neck strangled him and broke his neck. By this time he was probably dead, but then his throat was cut. Finally he was placed face down in the peat.

52 There is some evidence that Viking warriors sacrificed (probably willing) slave girls to accompany their chiefs to the Afterlife.

14

Human sacrifice

53

The ancient Greeks did not practise human sacrifice, although it sometimes happens in Greek myths. In the story of the Trojan War, the Greek general Agamemnon was forced to sacrifice his daughter Iphigenia to the goddess Artemis. (In one version of the story Iphigenia was saved at the last minute.)

54

Slaves were buried alive to serve their masters and mistresses in the Afterlife in the ancient Chinese Shang and Zhou dynasties.

55

Early Roman sacrificial victims have been found buried in the foundations of buildings. Perhaps they gave the buildings strength?

56

Self-sacrifice (cutting or piercing your own body so that it bled) was common among the Aztecs and was one way to offer blood to the gods.

57

To keep the sun moving across the sky, the Aztecs believed it needed to be nourished with the blood of sacrificial victims. Prisoners taken in battle would be killed on special occasions, sometimes in their thousands. They were thrown over a stone altar, their hearts were pierced with a special knife, then their bodies were thrown down the steep temple steps. Skulls were displayed outside the temple on racks.

Aztec knife. The handle is made of turquoise mosaic. 15th–16th century AD.

Animal sacrifice

58

The Ashvamedha (horse sacrifice) was one of the most important royal rituals of the Vedic (ancient Hindu) religion. It could only be carried out by a king.

The horse was sprinkled with water, then set free to roam for a year.

It was followed by one hundred young men who watched closely where it went. All the lands it went through then belonged to the king.

On its return the horse was bathed, anointed and decorated.

Gold coin showing the tethered horse used in the Ashvamedha ritual of King Kumaragupta I, around AD 415–50.

The horse was then tied to a stake with seventeen other animals attached to it and slaughtered.

The queen would spend the night with the dead animal before it was roasted the next day.

59

Sometimes Aztecs killed a dog at funerals so that the dog's soul could lead the soul of the dead person safely through the underworld.

60

In ancient Rome animals were frequently sacrificed to the gods as it was believed that this was the best way of keeping them happy. The demand for sacrificial animals (especially pigs and cattle) was so great that a special market selling them sprang up in Rome.

61

Making a sacrifice to the gods was a very important part of ancient Greek religion. A bull, sheep, goat, or other animal was led to the altar in a procession, then sacrificed. The bones and fat were offered to the gods – the humans ate the good meat themselves.

A young cow being led to the altar, from the South Frieze of the Parthenon. Around 438–432 BC.

A Greek sacrifice. The bones, fat and tail are burned on the altar for the gods. The edible meat is roasted for the humans to eat.

17

The Afterlife

62

The Greeks believed that Charon the ferryman took the souls of the dead across the River Styx to Hades, the underworld. But Charon had to be paid, or he would not row the soul over the river. So the Greeks put a coin in a dead person's mouth as payment. The far side of the river was guarded by the three-headed dog Cerberus.

Charon the ferryman, on a white-ground vase.

63

The Greek underworld took its name from the god Hades, who ruled it.

64

Ancient Romans also believed in Hades the underworld, but they called the god who ruled it Pluto. Charon still rowed souls across the river to be judged.

65

Two thousand years before the ancient Greeks, the ancient Sumerians believed that the dead were ferried across a river in a boat to the next world. This world was probably beneath the earth.

66

The Maya believed that there was an underworld with nine levels. Your soul had to undertake a dangerous journey through these levels after you died. The worst one was called Metnal and was ruled over by Ah Puch, the god of death. He is shown as a skeleton hung with bells.

67

The Aztecs believed in a well-ordered life after death in a place called Mictlan, which had nine different levels. The soul of a dead person would go to a different level according to how they had died. Death was just a gateway, and not to be feared at all. There were also special paradises just for children, for men who had died in battle and for women who had died in childbirth.

Statue of the Aztec god of the dead, Mictlantecuhtli. AD 1325–1521.

68

The ancient Egyptians believed that after death, your soul had to go on a journey through the underworld, a place full of terrifying monsters and many dangers. A copy of the Book of the Dead could help you through this journey by giving you the right spells to say. If you survived the journey your heart was weighed against a feather, which stood for 'right' or 'truth'. If it did not balance, then your soul was eaten by the fierce Devourer, part-crocodile, part-lion and part-hippopotamus.

Animal-headed demons guarding one of the gates to the Egyptian underworld.

Sinners run from Hell towards Kshitigarbha, who has the power to save them. China, late 9th–early 10th century AD.

A large Ming porcelain figure of an assistant to the judge of hell, made around AD 1522–1620.

69

A Chinese painting in the British Museum shows the Ten Buddhist Kings of Hell. The kings judge people's souls to see what they should be reborn as in their next life. There are six *gati* (ways of rebirth), in the following order:

1. Ways of divine beings
2. Titanic demons
3. Men
4. Animals
5. Hungry ghosts
6. Hell

70

When brave warriors died Vikings believed that their souls went to a big hall called Valhalla or 'Hall of the Slain'. Valhalla had 540 doors, walls made of spears and a roof made of shields. Every day the dead warriors fought mock battles, and every night they feasted.

71

The name 'Hell' is related to Hel in Norse mythology. Hel was the goddess of the underworld, which took her name. It was a miserable place, surrounded by a freezing river full of knives. The souls of the dead crossed over a bridge guarded by a giantess. In Hel they waded through rivers of blood, serpents' poison dripped on to them from the roof, and they could only drink goat's urine.

Tombs and graves

72

When the Sumerian Queen Pu-abi died, her corpse was richly dressed and laid on a wooden bier, with a gold cup by her hand. Teams of oxen harnessed to vehicles were then buried with her, as well as ninety attendants in their best clothes, laid out in rows. The Great Death Pit nearby also held six servants, four harpists and sixty-four other beautifully dressed women. They may have all taken poison, or were buried when they were already dead, or unconscious. Pu-abi was buried about 2600 BC in one of the royal graves found at Ur, Mesopotamia (modern Iraq).

Queen Pu-abi's golden headdress, made about 2600 BC.

73

The Hopewell people of North America lived around 100 BC in the area that is now Ohio. They were successful farmers who built large earthworks. Some of these may have been used to hold ceremonies, others are burial mounds where important people were laid to rest surrounded by tools and beautiful jewellery.

The Chinese thought that the Afterlife was rather like real life, and that a person could take objects with them if models of the things were left in their tomb. These could sometimes be life-sized.

Bullock pulling a cart, a tomb model from China, 6th century AD.

SEVEN FACTS
about Egyptian tombs

75 Most New Kingdom Egyptian rulers were buried in a place called the Valley of the Kings in fancy tombs cut into the rock.

76 Egyptian tombs were full of precious objects, models and pictures. Ancient Egyptians believed that people could use the things buried with them in the Afterlife. For example, model boats were buried to help the person's soul on its journey through the next world.

77 Offerings of food and drink were given to the dead. The Egyptians thought that the spirit of the person could eat the food if it was in their tomb.

Box of *shabtis* from the tomb of a woman called Henutmehyt, around 1250 BC.

78 Egyptians buried model servants called *shabtis* with the dead to serve them in the Afterlife.

79 Coffins and tombs were inscribed with hieroglyphic spells to help the dead person on their journey to paradise.

80 Tomb robbers, from ancient Egyptian times to the present day, have stolen the tomb goods from many Egyptian tombs.

81 The only Egyptian king's tomb to escape the tomb robbers was that of Tutankhamun.

Food offerings found in an Egyptian tomb.

82

Roman cemeteries had to be outside towns by law, mainly because of the risk of disease. Cemeteries were often laid out alongside main roads. On some days of the year offerings of food and drink were given to the dead – these could be put down tubes into the graves.

83

In Roman times, Christians and Jews and even some pagan Romans sometimes buried their dead in underground caves called catacombs. The Christian catacombs in Rome are the most famous. As well as providing cheap and plentiful graveyard space, the catacombs were used for meetings and ceremonies.

84

In Iron Age Britain, important people sometimes seem to have been buried with chariots. A fascinating woman was buried at Wetwang in Yorkshire. The woman was very tall for an Iron Age person, at 1.75 m (5 ft 9 in). She had a badly scarred face. She also had a dislocated shoulder, meaning that in real life she couldn't have actually driven the chariot she was buried in.

Powerful people were sometimes buried inside their ships in Anglo-Saxon England. The most famous of these burials is at Sutton Hoo in Suffolk. An oak ship, 27 metres (over 80 feet) long, was deeply buried beneath a large grassy mound. Inside the ship a dead man was laid, surrounded by his weapons and other precious objects. The ship rotted away, but the outline of her planks and iron rivets was preserved as an outline in the sandy soil.

The outline of the Sutton Hoo ship preserved in the sand, as it was found in 1939.

Helmet from the ship burial at Sutton Hoo in England, early 7th century AD.

Family life

86

The ancient Egyptian words for 'son' and 'daughter' were written with bird hieroglyphs and may really mean 'chick'.

| 'Son' | 'Daughter' |

90

Aztecs were very loving but very strict parents. Children could be severely punished if they misbehaved. This picture from an Aztec book shows a parent holding a child in the stinging smoke from a fire of chillies. Another punishment was pricking the child with cactus spines. We don't know if they really did anything so cruel!

87

The Egyptians valued children highly, and families often had between five and ten children, but the death rate among children was very high.

88

The Aztecs said that a baby was like a jewel or a precious flower. When an Aztec baby was born there were celebrations lasting several days.

89

Aztec children had several names. One name was always their birth date, such as One Flower. People thought the day decided the child's future. A child born on Two Rabbit might be a drunkard!

91 ELEVEN EGYPTIAN NAMES
and what they mean

Ramesses	The sun god has given birth to him
Aapehty	Great of strength
Meresankh	May she love life
Wereshunefer	The one who spends the day happy
Dersenedj	The one who wards away fear
Desheri	Red
Anemher	Gorgeous
Webennesiah	The moon shines for her
Bia	Miracle
Meretites	She who loves her father
Seshen	Lotus flower (an ancient Egyptian version of the modern name Susan).

92 Vikings did not have surnames like ours. Instead they were named after their fathers and part of their names said whether they were his son or daughter. A family tree might look like this:

```
            Harald
              |
        Erik Haraldson
         ┌────┴────┐
Astrid Eriksdaughter   Olaf Erikson
```

93
Roman fathers literally owned the rest of the family and made all the decisions.

94

In ancient Athens, a woman was expected to look after the home and have children. Women could not inherit property. So if a woman had no brothers, when her father died she might have to marry her father's brother to keep the estate in the family.

Mother and child from a Ming dynasty woodblock print, 17th century AD.

A small child crawling towards its mother, on a Greek pot.

95

Chinese ages were counted from one rather than zero, so Chinese babies were considered to be one year old the day they were born. They would then add a year to their age at the next Chinese New Year, instead of having a birthday (this meant that a child born on New Year's Eve could be two years old the next day!).

96

FIVE ANGLO-SAXON NAMES
and what they mean

Gertrude	Spear strength
Alfred	Elf counsel
Hilda	Battle maid
Edward	Guardian of wealth
Unready	Badly advised, 'without counsel' (as in King Ethelred the Unready)

An Anglo-Saxon home.

Wedding bells

97 Roman marriages were mostly arranged by families. Women had very little say in the decision about who they married. They were often given as brides aged as young as twelve to much older men.

98 Girls of thirteen or fourteen were married to men of about thirty in ancient Greece, although women in Sparta had more equality and probably married when they were older.

Carving of a Roman wedding ceremony.

A Greek wedding procession, painted on a vase.

99 *During the Ptolemaic period in Egypt (332–30 BC), kings married their sisters and declared that they were goddesses.*

100 *When a young Maya man got married, he would work for his wife's family for about six years. After this the couple went to live with or near the husband's family.*

101 *In ancient China a man could have only one main wife. She shared his honours. But he was also free to take lesser wives, called concubines, to ensure he had more children. He could have many concubines. These second-class wives could be very badly treated by their husband and the chief wife.*

A Chinese lady waiting for her husband to arrive. Qing dynasty hanging scroll, 19th century AD.

102

In ancient China, marriages were arranged by professional matchmakers, sometimes before the bride and groom were even born! A bride had to become a member of her husband's family, obeying his parents totally and worshipping his ancestors, and she was expected to provide children, especially sons.

Mother and children playing in a garden. An 18th-century Chinese hanging scroll.

Divorce

103

A man could divorce his wife for practically anything in ancient China, even talking too much. However, he couldn't divorce her if she had no family home to return to.

104

In ancient Mesopotamia a man could divorce his wife, or take another wife, if the first wife didn't have any children. Children could also be adopted.

105

A divorced wife in ancient Egypt was entitled to some support from her ex-husband, whatever the circumstances. This support was sometimes laid down in a contract when the marriage took place, and could be as much as a third of the marriage settlement.

A papyrus marriage contract from Egypt, 172 BC.

Work

106

Children as young as seven were given grown-up tasks in ancient China, such as helping their parents to grow food and support the family.

107

The birth of a girl to a poor family in ancient China was full of worry. The family would have to find the money to feed her, then find a dowry (a payment to her husband's family when she got married) for her. To help earn money, Chinese girls learned how to weave and spin cloth.

108

Girls in ancient Egypt learned how to look after the home. Boys worked in the fields with their fathers.

109

Aztec boys were taught trades by their fathers, often when they were very young. They could be sent out fishing on their own from about the age of fourteen.

110

The best job for a boy in Egypt was to become a government scribe. Egyptian parents wanted this for their sons more than anything else as it gave them the most power and wealth.

A statue of an Egyptian scribe with his papyrus across his knees. Around 750 BC.

111

Aztec girls were taught how to do household tasks such as weaving or sweeping the floor by their mothers and aunts.

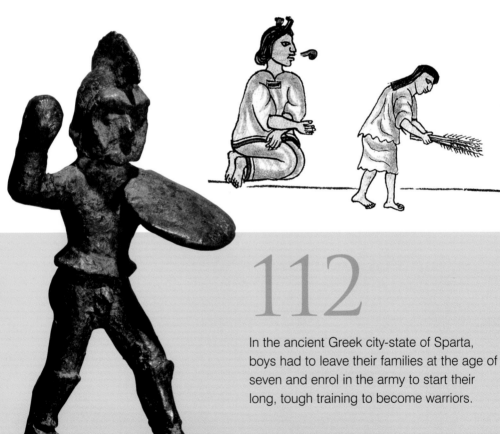

112

In the ancient Greek city-state of Sparta, boys had to leave their families at the age of seven and enrol in the army to start their long, tough training to become warriors.

A bronze figure of a fierce Spartan warrior.

School

113 SIX SCHOOL SUBJECTS

studied by boys in Athens

READING
WRITING
MEMORISING THE WORKS OF HOMER
PLAYING THE LYRE
SINGING
FITNESS AND GYMNASTICS

Boy learning to ride a horse, shown on a Greek pot.

114

Only rich Roman boys went to school. As well as reading and writing, they also learned how to be good soldiers. Schools were very strict and pupils were often beaten.

115

Only boys from some rich families went to school in ancient Egypt. The first thing they learned was how to write government documents. They spent hours copying long, boring lists.

Clay tablet with schoolwork, Old Babylonian, about 1900–1700 BC.

116

Boys from a few scribal families went to school in ancient Babylon. They learned how to write cuneiform script on clay tablets.

33

117

Education was highly prized in ancient China. Chinese civil servants had to write a poem to qualify for the job. Literary exams for the civil service started in the Han dynasty (206 BC–AD 220).

A Chinese official writing in his study.

118

Aztec boys from ordinary families went to 'houses of youth', schools where they learned skills such as carpentry, fishing or weaving. The children of the nobility were taught in schools run by priests. The boys learned astronomy, maths, architecture and history.

Boy learning to fish, from an Aztec book.

Keeping clean

119

Most Aztec homes had their own bathhouse, called a *temazcalli*, which was a bit like a modern sauna. The whole family used this every day.

120

The ancient Egyptians went to the river to wash themselves and their clothes. Only the very rich had bathrooms and toilets.

121

The Greeks had no toilets at home. Instead they used chamber pots.

122

Most Romans went to public bathhouses every day to wash. These were very sociable places where people would meet up with their friends.

123

The Anglo-Saxons had surprisingly good teeth, because there was no sugar in their diet. Cures for toothache were based on herbs. They also used charms and amulets.

124

To get clean after exercise, ancient Greek athletes smeared olive oil on themselves, then scraped it off with a strigil, bringing the dirt away with it.

Bronze figure of a boy using a strigil.

Teeth

125

Some Roman toothpaste recipes included human urine.

126

The ancient Egyptians did not have toothbrushes, but grit and straw in their bread acted as a toothbrush. As a result, the Egyptians generally had very few cavities. A bigger problem was that because of the grit in their bread, their teeth wore down, sometimes so quickly that they became damaged and infected. This was very painful, and could even lead to death.

Fashion

127

The Celts (who lived in western Europe from around 700 BC) used the plants around them to dye their clothes different colours. These included:

birch bark (brown)
goose grass root (red and orange)
berries (blues and purples).

128

One Anglo-Saxon monk described well-off women's fashions: they wore colourful tunics, with silk borders on the sleeves and head-dresses, and red leather shoes. They had long veils on their heads; they curled their hair, and sharpened their finger-nails like hawk's claws.
Do you think he approved?

129

Viking helmets didn't have horns on them! Neither did those of the Celtic peoples as a rule, though one unusual horned Celtic helmet has been found in the River Thames.

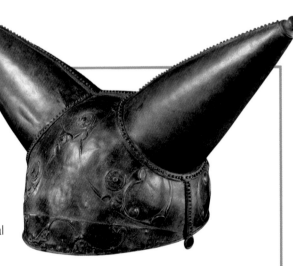

Helmet found in the River Thames, London, England, 150–50 BC.

130

Silk is a beautiful, light, shimmering material that has been made in China for about 6,000 years. The silk travelled thousands of miles along the 'Silk Road' (a network of roads and sea routes) to reach Europe. It wasn't until the sixth century AD that European spies discovered that silk was made from the cocoons of silkworm moths.

131

Many Chinese scholars would grow their fingernails long to show that they were too clever and scholarly to do manual work. Some would leave just one fingernail long. The empress dowager Ci Xi (AD 1835–1908) grew each fingernail to about twice as long as her hands.

Chinese lady in flowing silk clothes, with a phoenix, painted on a silk hanging scroll. Ming dynasty.

132

The Ainu people of the island of Hokkaido, Japan used to weave clothes out of bark. The men would collect the bark from young trees, soften it in water, separate out the fibres and dry it in the sun. The women would then weave it into clothes.

133

Folding fans were invented in Japan in the fourth century AD.

Woodblock print of a Japanese actor holding a folding fan.

134

The Maya of Mexico wore clothes woven from cotton and dyed. Other body ornaments, such as headdresses, could be made from fibres softened from the bark of trees.

135

A *quechquemitl* was a simple neck cape worn by Mexican women. It was triangular in shape, sometimes decorated with tassels, and probably had bold, brightly coloured designs.

The Aztec goddess Chalchiuhtlicue wears a *quechquemitl*.

136

Children in ancient Egypt sometimes wore no clothes at all as it was so hot. Most of the time they wore simple tunics.

137

Only Roman citizens were allowed to wear the toga. A toga was basically a large blanket shaped like a semi-circle. This was draped over one arm, leaving the other one free. It must have been quite cumbersome to wear.

138

In ancient Egypt people often wore sandals made from papyrus (a kind of reed). Only rich people could afford leather sandals.

139 HOW TO DRESS IN A TOGA

1 Hold the toga behind you. Hook one pointed end over your shoulder so it hangs down in front of you to the ground.

2 Take the other pointed end, bring it around loosely in front of you and put it over the same shoulder, tucking it in firmly behind.

3 Drape the other end over your arm.

4 Strut around looking important.

Bronze statuette of a Roman *lictor*, or magistrate, wearing a toga.

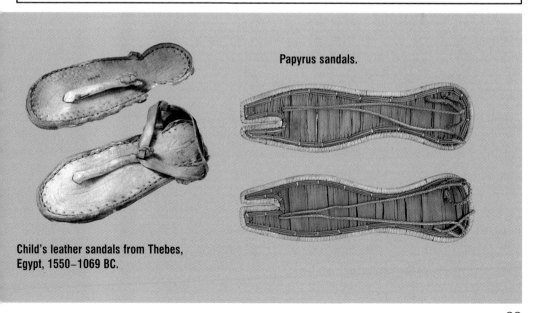

Papyrus sandals.

Child's leather sandals from Thebes, Egypt, 1550–1069 BC.

140

Ancient Romans had many different types of shoes. Soldiers wore sturdy sandals with hobnails hammered into the soles to make them stronger. Workmen wore tough shoes. Richer people had beautiful slippers specially made for them.

141

Ancient Egyptian men and women wore loincloths as underwear. King Tutankhamun had 145 loincloths buried with him in his tomb, to wear during his eternal Afterlife.

142

The ancient Greeks wore clothes made mainly of linen (made from fibres of the flax plant) and of wool.

143

Greek women often wore *peploi*. A *peplos* was a long piece of material folded in two and pinned together at the shoulders. It was tied around the waist with a belt.

Jewellery

144

Amazing objects made of sheets of gold have been found near the capital of the old kingdom of Silla in Korea. Gold crowns, belts, earrings, necklaces, vessels, and even gold shoes have been excavated.

Pair of Silla dynasty gold earrings from Korea, 5th–6th centuries AD.

Anglo-Saxon brooch with garnet cloisonné decoration, late 6th or early 7th century AD.

147

Aztecs wore ornaments made of gold, pottery and obsidian (black volcanic glass) in pierced ears, noses and lips.

148

The Celts from Iron Age Britain were among the most skilful metalworkers in the world. They made necklaces called torcs, often made of several strands of metal twisted together. These could be very heavy – the gold Great Torc found at Snettisham weighs over a kilogram (over two pounds). No wonder, as it is made from sixty-four separate threads.

145

The Anglo-Saxons used brooches to fasten their loose-fitting clothes. Brooches looked pretty and also stopped garments from falling off.

146

Wealthy Anglo-Saxon women wore beautiful jewellery, and men sometimes owned weapons with lots of decoration. The Anglo-Saxons especially liked using red stones called garnets and are famous for a highly skilled technique called garnet cloisonné, in which red garnets were placed into a delicate mesh of gold threads.

Great Torc from Snettisham, Norfolk, England, about 100 BC.

41

Hair and head-dresses

149

Court ladies in ancient Sumer grew their hair into one long plait which they then wound around the head. They wore beautiful head-dresses of ribbons and beads, fixed on with pins.

150

Until they reached puberty at around 12 or 14, Egyptian children had shaved heads with just one plait of hair behind the ear. This was called a 'sidelock of youth' or 'Horus lock', after the god Horus, who is often shown as a child.

151

Hair conditioners and setting lotion were used by ancient Egyptians. Wealthy men and women wore wigs. In paintings, these are heavy and black but some surviving wigs show they were also made in lighter colours.

152

Aztec nobles wore big head-dresses made of coloured feathers and other precious materials, to indicate their rank.

Man's wig made of human hair, from Thebes, Egypt, 1550–1300 BC.

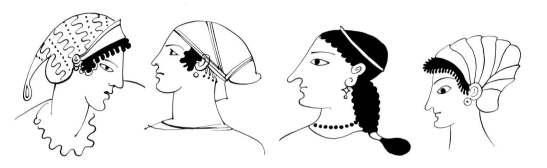

Some different hairstyles worn by women in ancient Greece.

153

Greek women wore their hair long and tied up. Only female slaves and those in mourning had short hair.

154

The emperor Hadrian (ruled AD 117–38) started the Roman fashion for beards in the second century AD. Until then beards had not been at all popular with Romans, although Greek men wore them.

Marble bust of Hadrian.

155

Chinese ladies wore elaborate high hairstyles, using false hair, and held in place by pins and combs of jade, gold, silver, glass and ivory.

Finely dressed Chinese lady with high hairdo, from a hanging scroll of the 9th century AD.

Make-up

156

Egyptian men and women wore black or green eye makeup, and the women also used red iron oxide to colour their cheeks, lips and nails.

157

Egyptians used cleansing creams and deodorants, and rubbed on perfumed oil to protect their skin from the sun.

158

Ancient Greek face whitener was made with lead and vinegar – very bad for the skin!

An Egyptian lady's make-up.

This make-up box belonging to Ahmose of Peniati contained black kohl for the eyes. From Thebes, Egypt, 1500–1440 BC.

159

Anglo-Saxons used to pluck out unwanted hair with metal tweezers.

Anglo-Saxon tweezers.

Food and drink

160

All the tea that we drink today comes from teas first grown and drunk in ancient China. Tea (*cha*) was drunk by rich and poor, and unusual kinds were tasted in tea-houses, a popular place to meet up with friends.

Jizhou tea bowl from China, AD 960–1279.

161

Because pomegranates are full to bursting with so many seeds, in ancient China they stood for a good luck wish for the birth of many sons.

A Roman model of a man ploughing with oxen.

162

Poor Romans ate bread, cheese, olives, beans, vegetables and cheap meats made into pies and sausages. The emperor gave many people who lived in the big cities free handouts of bread, olive oil and pork meat to eat because they were so poor.

163

Three meals a day, eaten by all Romans, rich or poor.
Breakfast: *ientaculum* (children often bought breakfast from a snack bar on the way to school)
Lunch: *prandium*
Dinner: *cena*

164

In the ancient Roman world, meat was either roasted or boiled. All meat was served with rich sauces, nearly all of which contained *garum* (also called *liquamen*). This was a sauce made from the intestines and heads and tails of fish, left out to go liquid in the sun. It sounds disgusting but actually tasted quite nice, a bit like Worcester sauce.

A Roman mosaic showing fish and fruit.

165

MENU FOR A RICH ROMAN'S DINNER PARTY

GUSTATIO *(appetisers)*
Eggs
Cheese
Snails fed on milk
Fish
Salad
Vegetables: asparagus, mushrooms, peas, beans, cabbage, carrots
Goose
Chicken
Dormouse (perhaps stuffed with mince, rolled in poppy seeds and honey)

MENSAE PRIMAE
(main course)
Ham
Venison
Wild Boar
Goat
Hare
Ostrich
Flamingo
Parrot (served with honey, dates and sesame seeds)

SECUNDAE MENSAE
(dessert)
Spiced cake
Egg custard
Pastries (flavoured with wine and honey)
Fruit: apples, plums, peaches, pears, grapes, figs, cherries

166

People ate bread with every meal in ancient Greece. Greeks ate fish and shellfish but not much meat. Sheep were kept for wool and milk, but they were very rarely eaten as they were too valuable. Honey was used as a sweetener, because there was no sugar.

Loaf of bread – probably a bit stale by now! – from Thebes, Egypt, around 1500 BC.

167

In ancient Egypt, the favourite food was bread and the favourite drink beer. People drank more beer than water.

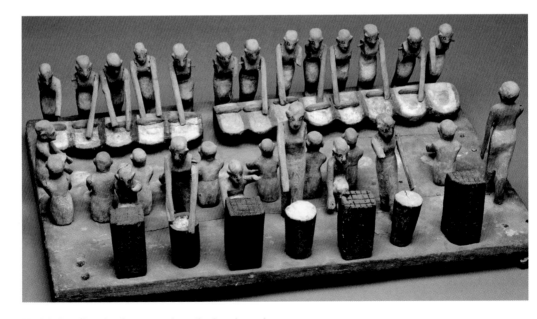

Model of an Egyptian brewery, where the female workers are busy grinding grain and making it into beer.

168

Ancient Egyptians bred ducks, geese and pigeons to eat, fattening them up on a diet of pellets of fat. They also ate a lot of fish, caught from the Nile, and from lakes and marshes. Only the very wealthy ate beef, as this was extremely expensive.

Cattle painted on the wall of the tomb-chapel of Nebamun.

169

There were no potatoes or tomatoes in ancient Egypt, Greece, or Rome. Potatoes and tomatoes were two of the plants that came from the Americas. Other foods that were introduced to Europe from Mexico include chocolate, maize, green peppers, chilli peppers, avocadoes, squash, vanilla and turkey.

170

There were no oranges or lemons in ancient Egypt, Greece or Rome. Lemons were brought to Italy by Arab traders about the second century AD. They came from the Himalayan area of north-east India. Oranges probably reached Europe about the ninth century AD. They came from Burma and south-west China, brought westwards by Arab traders.

The Maya young maize god, from Honduras, AD 600–800.

171

Maize (sweetcorn) was the main food of the Aztecs and Maya of ancient Mexico. It was ground between stones to make flour, which was then made into flat tortillas (pancakes). These were cooked over a hot fire and served with chilli and beans. Maize was so important that maize gods were worshipped. The Maya believed that the gods made the first humans from ears of corn.

172

Chocolate, made from cacao beans, was widely used by the Maya and Aztecs and then later introduced to Europe. The Aztecs drank their *chocolatl* bitter and flavoured with chillies, and they thought it provided energy and wisdom. They also used cacao beans as money.

173

Vikings used the resin from pine trees as a kind of chewing gum.

174

An Anglo-Saxon shopping list for a feast given by the king of Wessex:

10 jars of honey
20 hens
300 loaves
12 casks of Welsh ale
1 cask of butter
30 casks of clear ale
5 salmon
2 old oxen
20 pounds weight of hay
10 geese

How many people do you think were invited?

175 In Anglo-Saxon England, feasting was a social occasion. People drank ale from large drinking horns which could be passed round to all the guests.

Anglo-Saxon drinking horn from Taplow, Buckinghamshire, late 6th century AD.

An Anglo-Saxon feast.

Having fun

Music, dance, theatre

176 The first paid musicians came from ancient Sumer in the third millennium BC.

177 Dances to help with good harvests or success in hunting were performed by the ancient Maya of Mexico.

Wooden slit-drum or *teponaztli* from Aztec Mexico, AD 1325–1521.

178 The Aztecs had many different sorts of instruments, including trumpets, flutes and drums.

179

FIVE INSTRUMENTS
played in ancient Sumer

HARP	PIPE
LYRE	TAMBOURINE
DRUM	

A lyre from the city of Ur, about 2600–2400 BC.

180

FOUR THEATRE WORDS
that we get from the ancient Greeks

Scene (*skene*)   the background

Chorus   group of performers

Orchestra   large area where the chorus sang
                         and danced

Proscenium (*proskenion*) frame around the stage

**Greek figure of an actor from
Myrina, western Asia Minor
(modern Turkey), 2nd century BC.**

181

Beowulf is a famous Anglo-Saxon poem. It tells the story of how the 'grim and greedy' monster Grendel raids the king's hall at night, killing many warriors. Beowulf the warrior slays the monster, but the next night Grendel's terrifying mother comes looking for vengeance. Beowulf pursues her to her lair in the lake and kills her with his mighty sword.

182

The *Book of Songs* is probably the oldest record of pop music to be found anywhere in the world. It was put together by the Yue-fu, a group sent round the country by the emperor of China in 120 BC to report on which songs were popular.

183 Greek poetry was always read aloud with music. The Greeks liked their poetry to teach things, and this could lead to some rather odd verses – for example the poet Nicander left a set of poems listing antidotes to poison and explaining how to cure animal bites.

184 Theatres first appeared in ancient Greece. Greek drama first developed out of songs and dances performed at religious festivals for the god Dionysus.

185 In Greek myth, Orpheus sang and played so beautifully that his music could even tame wild beasts.

186

Many Roman plays were borrowed from ancient Greece. Other plays, based on Roman humour, could get extremely rowdy, with actors and the audience shouting at each other during performances.

Actors in Greek comedies wore masks and padded costumes. This Greek pot shows a scene from a comic play.

Toys and games

187 Children in ancient Greece played on swings and seesaws.

188

Children played with rag dolls with real hair in ancient Egypt. Archaeologists have found model soldiers, houses and wooden animals in Egyptian tombs, but they may not be toys. The models may be for the use of the dead person in the afterlife.

Wooden cat with moving mouth from Egypt, 1550–1070 BC.

189 A team game of leapfrog called *khuzza lawizza* was played by ancient Egyptian children.

190 Patolli was a popular Aztec board game. Players raced their markers around a board painted on to a mat. Beans marked with dots were used as dice.

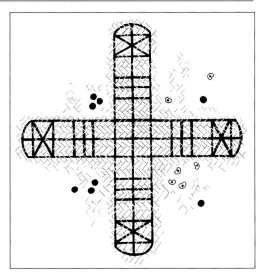

An Aztec patolli board.

191 Chess is the most successful board game ever invented. It probably began in India well over 1,000 years ago. The rules have changed slightly. Originally the queen used to be called the vizier. The piece could not move very far.

192 Mancala is an ancient game, still very popular today across Africa and the Caribbean. There are many versions, but they all involve players 'sowing' seeds or stones into rows of holes and trying to capture their opponent's pieces. It can be played extremely fast and furiously.

193

Pachisi board and pieces from Sri Lanka, 19th century AD.

Ludo – you have probably played it yourself – was brought to Britain in the nineteenth century. But it is based on pachisi, a much older game which has been popular in India for hundreds of years. Ludo is a simplified version, and is easier to play.

A mancala board from Sierra Leone, 20th century AD.

56

194 The ancient Egyptians loved playing board games. The most popular was called senet. A number of counters had to be moved around and off the board, a bit like modern backgammon. Senet was also played for religious reasons, as it was supposed to mirror the journey taken by the soul through the Afterlife.

Ivory senet board, with a drawer underneath to hold the pieces. Made between 1550 and 1069 BC.

195 The Anglo-Saxons probably played a game called *tabula*, which was like backgammon. They also enjoyed playing *latrunculi* (soldiers) a game where you tried to capture your opponent's army.

196 Young women and children in ancient Greece played *astragaloi* or knucklebones. Today we call the game jacks, or firestones. The pieces were the knuckle-bones of sheep or goats, or copies of these.

197 Romans played an early version of backgammon called *ludus duodecim scriptorum*. Rude messages between opponents were sometimes written on the boards! For example:

LEVATE	DALOCU	Get up	give me room
LUDERE	NESCIS	To play	you know nothing
IDIOTA	RECEDE	Idiot	push off!

Small terracotta figures of two Greek women playing knucklebones. From the Hellenistic Period, around 300 BC.

198 One of the oldest surviving board games in the world is the Royal Game of Ur. A version of this has been found scratched out next to the feet of the huge stone winged bull which guarded the gates of the city of Khorsabad. Perhaps the gate guards got bored and started a game.

199 One early popular use of kites across Asia was for fighting. Fighting kites were mostly small, flat paper kites, which were very agile. Part of their flying line was very rough, and this would be flown across an opponent's line to cut it and bring the kite down.

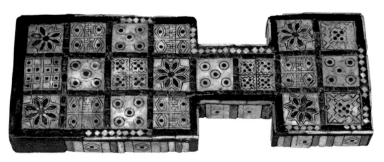

Board and pieces for the Royal Game of Ur, from the city of Ur in ancient Sumer. 2600–2400 BC.

200 Kites were probably invented in China. Their first-ever mention is in a 2,000-year-old story. One version tells how a tiny general called Han Xin (who died in 196 BC) tied himself to a kite and flew over the emperor's palace.

Kites were originally often used for military purposes, such as to measure distance. A more likely version of Han Xin's story is that he flew the kite (without being attached to it) over the palace and marked the length of the string. He then dug a tunnel to exactly the same length under the palace walls, and launched a surprise attack.

Art

201

There were many statues of emperors and gods in Roman towns and temples. Those that have survived are of white marble. When they were made they would have been painted in very bright colours, but by now all the paint has worn off.

202

A bright blue paint known as Maya blue was used by the Maya of ancient Mexico in their wall paintings. How this beautiful colour was made was a secret for thousands of years. Experts now think it is a mixture of indigo, clay and tiny metal particles that make the colour brighter.

203

The Nasca people of Peru lived between around 200 BC and AD 600. They created the mysterious Nasca lines, giant drawings on the desert floor of animals and geometric shapes. Some are over 100 metres (300 feet) long and can only be seen properly from the air.

204

When the famous *discobolus* (discus thrower) sculpture in the British Museum was restored, the head was put on back to front – it should be facing back towards the discus! Ancient Greek sculptors liked to give their statues as perfect bodies as possible.

Marble *discobolus* from the emperor Hadrian's villa. A Roman copy of a Greek bronze statue.

59

Inventions

The calendar

205

In ancient Rome the number of months in a year = 10

This division of a year was said to be invented by Romulus, the founder of Rome, in 753 BC. It was based on the Greek calendar, which followed the phases of the moon.

206

Days in a Roman year = 365

The Roman dictator Julius Caesar proclaimed in 45 BC that from that time onward there would be 365 days in a year, with an extra day in February every four years (a leap year).

Bust of Julius Caesar, from what is now Turkey. AD 50.

207

The Romans counted dates inclusively, which means they counted the day they started on as one, not zero. So 2nd–5th September would have been four days for the Romans. This can make working out dates in Roman documents very difficult. It also meant that after Julius Caesar reformed the calendar, the Roman government added a leap year every three years instead of every four years. It was thirty-six years before the emperor Augustus finally put this right.

208

Months in a year after Julius Caesar reformed the calendar = 12
These kept their old names of:

IANUARIUS
FEBRUARIUS
MARTIUS
APRILIS
MAIUS
IUNIUS
QUINTILIS (later became 'Iulius', named after Julius Caesar)
SEXTILIS (later became 'Augustus', named after the Emperor Augustus)
SEPTEMBER
OCTOBER
NOVEMBER
DECEMBER

209

Months in a year renamed by the emperor Charlemagne
Charlemagne (AD 742–814) renamed all of the months in Old German to describe the farming year. Starting from modern January, they are:

Wintarmanoth (winter month)
Hornung (spring)
Lentzinmanoth (Lent month)
Ostarmanoth (Easter month)
Winnemanoth (grazing month)
Brachmanoth (ploughing month)
Heuvimanoth (hay month)
Aranmanoth (harvest month)
Witumanoth (wood month)
Windumemanoth (vintage month)
Herbistmanoth (autumn/harvest month)
and Heilagmanoth (holy month).

210

Anglo-Saxon months of the year = 10
Starting from modern January, they are:

Solomnath (month of cakes. Offerings were made to the gods)
Hrethmonath (month of the goddess Hretha)
Eosturmonath (month of the goddess Eostre. This was at around the same time as Easter. We have taken the festival directly from the Anglo-Saxons)
Thirmilci (month in spring when cows are milked three times a day because the grass is lush)
Litha (month of the moon, around midsummer)
Weodmonath (month of weeds)
Haligmoanath (holy month. This is when harvest festivals were held, in late summer and early autumn)
Wintirfyllith (the first full moon of winter)
Blotmonath (blood month, when animals had to be killed for winter food)
Giuli (yuletide. This lasted for two months, including the winter solstice festival)

211

Days of the week = 7 (and their Roman and Anglo-Saxon pagan roots)

SUNDAY (day of the sun)
MONDAY (day of the moon)
TUESDAY (Tiw's day. Tiw was the god of war)
WEDNESDAY (Woden's day. Wodin was chief of the gods)
THURSDAY (Thor's day. Thor was god of thunder)
FRIDAY (Freya's day. Freya was the wife of Woden)
SATURDAY (Saturn's day. Saturn was the Roman god of agriculture)

212

The Anglo-Saxons thought the new day began at sunset on the day before. So after sunset Saturday would actually be called Sunnanniht (Sunday night), becoming Sunnandæg (Sunday) with the sunrise.

213

The ancient Egyptians had a ten hour day for practical purposes, although in some texts they described a twenty-four hour day. They had clocks, including sand and water clocks, to help them tell the time.

214

The Aztecs had two calendars, one for living and working by, the other for religious rituals. Each day was ruled over by a god. A giant image of the calendar was carved on a big stone in the central square of the capital Tenochtitlan. The calendar was also recorded on folding books made of deerskin.

215

The Egyptians thought that some days were lucky and others unlucky, and they looked at a calendar like the one on this papyrus to check before they planned anything. The bad days are written in red hieroglyphs. An example of a bad day: 'Do not go out on this day … whoever is born on this day will die through a serpent'.

216

Signs of the zodiac = 12

It was probably the Babylonian astrologers in the first millennium BC who thought of dividing the year into the twelve signs of the zodiac, based on star constellations they could see in the sky. How the sun moved through these was used to predict what would happen on earth. The signs as we know them today are taken from their ancient Latin names.

The signs of the zodiac are:
 ARIES (ram)
 TAURUS (bull)
 GEMINI (twins)
 CANCER (crab)
 LEO (lion)
 VIRGO (maiden)
 LIBRA (scales)
 SCORPIO (scorpion)
 SAGITTARIUS (archer)
 CAPRICORN (goat)
 AQUARIUS (water-bearer)
 PISCES (fish)

217

Ophiuchus (the serpent-bearer) is actually the thirteenth constellation that the sun passes through during the year. It comes after Scorpio and before Sagittarius. However, it does not have a sign of the zodiac to go with it.

218

The Maya calendar was based on observing the stars and planets and doing sums. It was astonishingly accurate. The Maya worked out the cycle of Venus for over 6,000 years with only one day's error.

THE TWELVE ANIMALS
of the Chinese zodiac

219

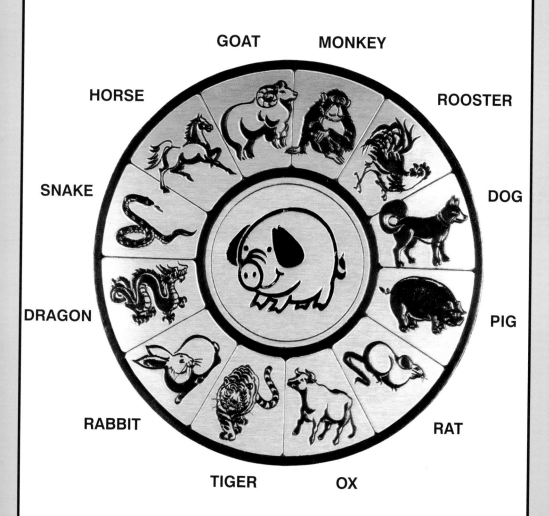

2007 is the year of the Pig according to the Chinese calendar.

Transport

220

The Aztecs had no transport with wheels at all – they just had wheels on a few toys.

221

The Aztecs had no pack animals to carry heavy things. Loads were carried by the people themselves, or by their slaves if they were lucky. The Aztecs were amazed to see the Spanish invaders riding horses.

222

The ancient Maya, like the Aztecs, did not have wheeled vehicles and so they walked everywhere. Rich nobles were carried around in litters, and traders also made journeys by canoe.

223

The Maya had a very big road system linking their cities which was also used for processions and journeys to special religious places.

Model of a boat from ancient Egypt, about 1900 BC.

224

Viking longship.

The Vikings travelled in longships. These crafts were built of overlapping planks with a single square sail. They were very sturdy in rough seas. The sailors kept their possessions in trunks and sat on them to row. The Vikings gave their ships names such as Strider, Crane, Long Serpent or Bison.

225

Egyptians often travelled by boat. The River Nile flowed south to north so they rowed in this direction. To come back they hoisted a sail to take advantage of the wind blowing north to south.

226

In ancient Greece most people walked to get around. Carriages and horses were only for the rich. Peasants might own a donkey.

228

The ancient Egyptians mostly used donkeys for transport. Horses were only used by the very rich. Camels were not used until very late in Egyptian history.

227

Most cargo in ancient Greece (such as oil or wine) was carried in large pottery jars called amphorae. Cargo often went by ship around the coast of Greece or between the islands.

In the middle of this Greek cup a man is lifting an amphora. Cargo ships sail around the edge of the cup.

Technology

229

There were only a very few paved roads in ancient Greece. Most roads were just very rough tracks.

230

To get from town to town most Romans used covered wagons or carts. They were covered in cloth with seats on top. They were bumpy, slow, and very uncomfortable.

231

Roman roads 'cut through mountains and eliminated the bends', as it said on a Roman milestone in Germany. They were the best roads ever seen.

232

Corn from Egypt arrived in the Roman empire on huge boats, the supertankers of the ancient world.

233

Tool-making began in East Africa about 2.4 million years ago. Early humans began to shape the tools they needed, instead of just picking up sticks or sharp-edged stones. They discovered that by using a hard stone as a hammer, they could knock flakes off both sides of a pebble to create sharp edges. These tools could be used to chop branches from trees or cut meat from large animals.

Paleolithic stone chopping tools from Tanzania, Africa, about 1.8 million years old.

234

Water clocks were invented thousands of years ago in China. They started out as a series of jars which would each empty after a set time.

235

In China during the Tang dynasty (AD 618–907), canals were built to bring water to distant areas to help in the growing of rice, the main food crop. The water was brought up to the fields by a clever chain-and-paddle system worked by turning a crank.

Rice fields in China. This watercolour was painted in China in the 19th century AD for export to Europe.

236

The Great Wall of China was built in the third century BC, on the orders of Zheng of the Qin, the First Emperor of China, as a defence against invading tribes. It was an amazing 6,000 kilometres (4,000 miles) long. Watchtowers were built every few hundred metres. The wall we see today was heavily restored during the Ming dynasty (AD 1368–1644).

237

The Chinese discovered how to make porcelain in the sixth century AD, more than 1,000 years before the Europeans managed to invent it. Porcelain was very popular in Europe, and lots of porcelain items were imported from China.

Porcelain flask made in China for export to Spain, AD 1573–1620.

TEN THINGS
THAT THE ROMANS DID FOR US

The Romans had by far the most advanced technology of their times. Many Roman inventions and introductions were lost after the downfall of the empire, and were not rediscovered for many centuries.

238 Lighthouses: Romans built them at the entrances to many harbours. Egyptians and Greeks first used lighthouses, and the Romans brought lighthouses to Britain (you can see the remains of one at Dover).

239 Cranes: enormous cranes to help with building work were powered by slaves walking round inside huge wheels.

240 Glass-blowing: this technique meant glass could be mass produced, so you no longer had to be very rich to afford it.

Blown glass jug from Roman Britain, 2nd century AD.

241 Plumbing: the Romans invented aqueducts and lead pipes for moving water around. They built the longest known tunnel – it was 5.6 km (3.5 miles) long – to drain a lake.

242 Concrete: the strength and lightness of Roman concrete made possible great domes, bridges, arches and aqueducts that could not have been built from stone. (They also knew that adding horsehair made concrete less likely to shrink, and adding blood made it resistant to frost.)

243 Transport: Roman roads were used for up to 1,000 years after the empire ended. At their peak they covered a total of 85,000 km (53,000 miles). Changing stations could enable a courier to cover nearly 800 km (500 miles) in 24 hours using a relay of horses.

244 Central heating: the Romans used a clever system of underfloor heating, called the hypocaust, to heat rooms in the public baths and in the villas of wealthy people.

245 Farming: harvesting machines invented by the Romans were not bettered until the nineteenth century.

246 Maths: the abacus, probably invented in Mesopotamia, was the first portable counting machine ever. The Romans introduced it to Britain.

247 Architecture: the Roman arch was perfected, and the impressive roof dome was invented (as in the Pantheon).

Medicine and illness

248

The oldest prescriptions in the world, dating from about 3000 BC, have been found on a clay tablet from ancient Sumer. They explain how to make a poultice for a wound from parts of plants crushed together with oil, and how to make medicines from natural ingredients such as shells, beer, plants, salt and ashes.

249

The people of Sumer thought that most of the causes of illness were supernatural and were the result of curses, the will of the gods, or witchcraft.

They had two types of doctor: the *asoo*, who administered practical remedies; and the *ashipu*, a magician who used spells.

These would often work together to cure a patient.

250

The Greek Hippocrates is known as the father of modern medicine. He was the first person to observe the patient carefully and try to come up with a diagnosis without being influenced by superstition. He is probably the most famous doctor of all time. Some modern doctors swear the Hippocratic Oath, named after him.

251

Many of the ancient Greeks believed that you could only be well if you had the right balance of the four humours in your body. The humours were:

    black bile
    yellow bile
    blood
    phlegm.

For this reason, doctors often advised vomiting or blood-letting to restore the body's balance.

A Greek doctor examines a boy with a swollen stomach. On the right is a cupping vessel, used to draw blood or pus. The vessel is shown much larger than it would be in real life.

252

Asklepios was the doctor god of ancient Greece. A cult grew up around him. Patients slept in his temples hoping to be sent a dream which would tell them what would cure them.

Marble head of Asklepios.

253

The ancient Egyptians liked using dung to treat a whole range of illnesses. This included the dung of crocodiles, pelicans and lizards. They even used human poo for some ailments.

254

The Babylonians thought that toothache was caused by a worm.

73

255

Hoping to be cured, Greeks and Romans left carved models of their afflicted body parts in temples dedicated to Asklepios. Large numbers of model legs, feet, arms, eyes and ears have been found.

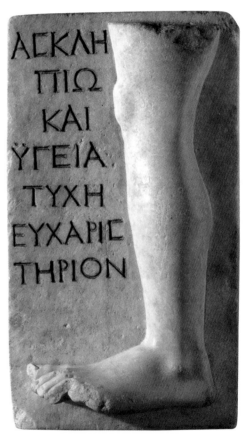

Terracotta models of an eye and ear.

A thank-you to Asklepios for making a leg better, left in a temple on the island of Milos, Greece, AD 100–200.

256

The disease tuberculosis was around in ancient Egyptian times. It was caught from drinking milk or eating meat from infected cows, and shows up in damage to the spine. This can be seen in some Egyptian mummies.

257

Between 430 and 426 BC, Athens suffered outbreaks of a terrible plague, which killed almost a third of the population. Symptoms included:

SHAKING
SORES AND ULCERS COVERING THE BODY
VOMITING
A BLEEDING MOUTH AND THROAT, then
DEATH.

The illness was probably brought in from north Africa on overcrowded boats.

258

The ancient Egyptians had remedies for common health problems. One remedy for a skin complaint contained aloe vera (a plant which we still use today for the skin), cucumber and wine. Pigs' teeth and tortoise bile were used in other remedies. However, Egyptians thought that these would only work if used with the right magic spells.

259

The perfectly preserved body of a head louse was found in the hair of an Egyptian who died 5,000 years ago. Remedies for oily lotions to get rid of head lice are found in ancient Egyptian texts.

Silver coin from Cyrene showing a silphium plant.

260

The Greek city of Cyrene (now in modern Libya) flourished because of its trade in a plant called silphium. Silphium was used in cooking, and also to treat many ailments including sickness, colds and headaches. Today we don't know exactly what silphium was, so we cannot test it for ourselves.

261

Viking men and women both had long hair. Combs were probably used to remove head lice, not just to make hair look tidy.

263

Dung was used to cure a large number of ailments In ancient Rome. The Roman writer Pliny listed a whole range of dung treatments, including eating mouse poo to sweeten bad breath.

262

Doctors in ancient Rome were able to amputate arms and legs and set bones. They learned a great deal about surgery from the Egyptians and the Greeks. Archaeologists have found many beautifully-crafted surgical instruments from Rome.

Some Roman surgical instruments.

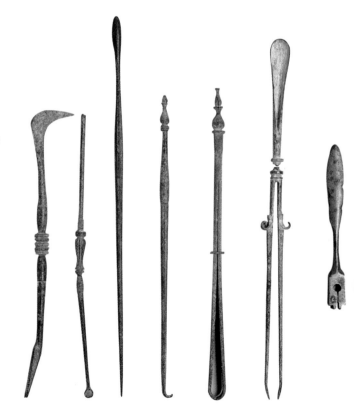

264

Some oculists (specialist eye doctors) in ancient Rome could operate on such problems as in-growing eyelashes. This was without anaesthetic (not invented until the nineteenth century), and without proper cleanliness, so many patients died.

265

Anglo-Saxons thought that eating goat's fat was a good treatment for dysentery.

266

The later Anglo-Saxons believed that wine, sometimes warmed up or spiced, had medicinal qualities.

267

In ancient China people believed that sickness was brought on by an evil wind. They wore charms and amulets to ward off the bad spirits that caused this, or even had the spirits exorcised (driven out).

268

The mythical Emperor Shennang (ruled about 5,000 years ago) was known as the father of Chinese farming. He is believed to have written 365 herbal, mineral and animal remedies in a manual. Some of these are still used today, such as rhubarb, which helps relieve constipation.

Eye-doctor's stamp used for marking ointments, from Roman Britain, 1st–4th century AD.

269

It was not allowed for male doctors to touch female patients in ancient China, so instead they used dolls on which the patient could point out which part was hurting.

270

Acupuncture was invented in China and practised from about 2700 BC. It is still in use today. It is based on the theory that energy moves through the body and can be rebalanced using needles stuck gently into the correct pathways.

271

Buddhist monks in India had to carry five simple medicines wherever they went, including fresh butter, molasses and honey.

272

Cutting off the nose was a punishment in ancient India. Doctors worked out how to rebuild noses using skin cut from the cheek, with tubes of reeds to keep the nostrils open. This is one of the earliest known types of plastic surgery.

273

The Black Death first swept across Europe in the mid-fourteenth century, killing between one-third and two-thirds of the population. At the same time similar epidemics attacked Asia and the Middle East. The plague returned frequently until the 1700s, hitting London particularly hard in 1666. The most common form was the bubonic plague, where victims had large pus-filled swellings and dark blotches on their bodies. The Black Death had a huge effect on the way people thought about death, religion and each other.

The Rich Man, from the Dance of Death series of paintings by Holbein, shows that death does not care how much money you have. AD 1526.

Rulers

EGYPTIAN PHARAOHS

274 Each Egyptian pharaoh had five official names: his own birth name, and four others which he chose when he took the throne. The full name of Ramesses II translates as (take a deep breath):

Strong Bull, Beloved of Maat
Protector of Egypt and Curber of Foreign Lands
Powerful of Years, Great of Successes
Powerful is the Justice of Ra
Ramesses.

275 Egyptian pharaohs were sometimes named after a famous earlier king. How many Egyptian pharaohs had the same name?

Ramesses = 11
Thutmose = 4
Amenemhat = 7
Amenhotep = 4
Cleopatra = 7
Ptolemy = 15

Statue of Amenhotep III, who ruled Egypt around 1390–1352 BC.

276

Pepi II was said to have ruled Egypt for a staggering ninety-four years! He was only six when he came to the throne, and was said to be the pharaoh who ruled the longest, from 2278 to 2184 BC. However, there is a lack of definite information about Pepi so we cannot be certain of these dates. The next contender is Ramesses II, the Great. We know he ruled for sixty-six years, from 1279 to 1213 BC.

Huge stone bust of Ramesses II, made around 1250 BC.

277 The youngest Egyptian pharaoh for whom we have definite records was Tutankhamun, who ascended the throne in 1336 BC at the tender age of nine. He was only seventeen when he died, possibly assassinated by a blow to the back of the head.

278 Ancient China was made up of many states, often at war with one another. The country was unified for the first time in 221 BC when King Zheng of Qin conquered his enemies and became the First Emperor. The English name for China comes from Qin, which is pronounced 'chin'.

The First Emperor of China.

Statue of the Assyrian king Ashurnasirpal II, 883–859 BC.

279 The Assyrian Empire stretched across northern Mesopotamia and was powerful in the first millennium BC. Ten names of Assyrian kings:

Ashuruballit
Tukulti-Ninurta
Ashur-dan
Adad-nirari
Ashurnasirpal
Tiglath-Pileser
Sargon
Sennacherib
Esarhaddon
Ashurbanipal

280

The most successful conqueror in history is probably Alexander the Great (356–323 BC). He was the first king of all Greece and his vast empire reached nearly to India. He only stopped his conquests when he got to India because his army refused to go any further. Alexander trained his huge war horse Bucephalus when he was only nine, and rode him into several battles.

281

Marble portrait of Alexander the Great, 2nd–1st century BC.

When Alexander, having reached India, decided to turn back westwards, the Indian ruler Chandragupta (ruled 322–298 BC) led an army to reclaim the lands Alexander had conquered. When Chandragupta had done this, he turned to the east and conquered lands there too. For the first time most of India was united under one powerful ruler. Later in his life Chandragupta gave up the throne to become a monk, and ended his days in deliberate semi-starvation.

282

Genghis Khan (AD 1162–1227) founded the largest empire in the history of the world, the Mongolian empire. Genghis Khan did this by uniting all the people of the steppes into a formidable army. In spite of popular belief, he was a politician rather than a marauder. He was good at military intelligence and made careful battle plans. Genghis Khan means 'Lord of the Earth'. His real name was Temujin.

283

The Viking ruler Eric Bloodaxe got his nickname when, as a young man in Norway, he murdered several of his brothers. From AD 947–954 he ruled part of England from Jorvik (York). Eric Bloodaxe often took time off from ruling to go and raid and murder in Scotland and Ireland. He was eventually killed in battle by the king of Wessex.

ROMAN EMPERORS

284

Romulus was the first ruler of Rome, according to legend. He and his brother Remus were said to have been left in the wild by their stepfather's wicked brother, and brought up by a she-wolf.

Silver coin showing Romulus and Remus with the she-wolf, made around 275–260 BC.

285

The maddest Roman emperor was probably Caligula (ruled AD 37–41). He sailed in jewel-encrusted ships equipped as floating palaces; he drank dissolved pearls; and infamously he even considered making his favourite racehorse a consul. Eventually, Caligula even thought himself a god. He dressed as one and demanded worship.

286

The Roman emperor Hadrian built a huge wall across the north of Britain to keep out the fierce tribes who lived in Caledonia to the north. Forts along the wall were manned by Roman soldiers, who must have found the weather very damp and cold.

287

Nero's reign (AD 54–68) started peacefully, but he gradually became more cruel and unpredictable. He forced people to watch him perform on stage for hours (and applaud enthusiastically), and he had thousands of people executed.

Statuette of Nero from Roman Britain, 1st century AD.

288 THE FIRST TEN
EMPERORS OF ROME
AND HOW THEY DIED

Being emperor was a very dangerous job. Many Roman emperors did not die peacefully.

AUGUSTUS: he may have died of natural causes, aged 71 (but there were rumours that his wife Livia had him poisoned)

TIBERIUS: natural causes, aged 77 (although there was a rumour that Caligula had him smothered)

CALIGULA: murdered by his own guards, aged 29

Cameo portrait of Augustus, made around AD 14–20.

Bronze head of Claudius, found in Britain, 1st century AD.

Marble head of Vespasian, made around AD 70–80.

CLAUDIUS: probably poisoned by his wife, Agrippina, aged 64

NERO: committed suicide after being deposed, aged 31

GALBA: ruled for only seven months before being killed, aged 72 and sick, by Otho's soldiers

OTHO: ruled for only three months before committing suicide, aged 37, after defeat by Vitellius

VITELLIUS: ruled for only eight months before being killed, aged 54, by Vespasian's troops

VESPASIAN: died of natural causes, aged 70

TITUS: died of a fever (though possibly poisoned by his doctor), aged 42

Britain

289

The legend of King Arthur comes from the time after the fall of the Roman empire when the Anglo-Saxons first started to invade Britain. The later medieval story tells how the British King Arthur, helped by his knights of the Round Table and the wizard Merlin, won many battles against Saxon invaders. There are older records of a warrior called Arthur from around this time, but his name is all we know for certain. There is no mention anywhere of Merlin or the knights.

290

Offa was the Anglo-Saxon king of Mercia (reigned AD 757–96). He probably built Offa's Dyke, a long earthwork along the Welsh borders, to keep out invaders and raiders from the west.

291

Alfred the Great, King of Wessex (reigned AD 871–99) is probably the most famous Anglo-Saxon king. At the start of his reign he had to retreat from the Vikings. There is a story that when he was hiding, a woman asked him to watch her cakes on the fire, but because he was a king he didn't know how to cook and let them burn. Eventually Alfred defeated the Vikings and ruled over most of England.

Silver penny of Alfred the Great, AD 871–99.

293

Moctezuma II, the Aztec emperor (AD 1502–20), had to face terrible problems during his reign. These included a plague of locusts, a famine and a flood. These were considered to be bad omens, and sure enough later in his reign the Spanish invaded, wiped out his government and murdered thousands of his people. Moctezuma was killed in the fighting.

292

King Cnut was such a powerful king that his followers told him he could even stop the tide coming in. So he went down to the beach and tried to stop the tide, possibly to show them they were wrong. Of course, he just got wet instead. But this story was first told long after Cnut died, and it probably never happened. Cnut was the first Viking to rule the whole of England, from AD 1016 to 1035. He was also king of Denmark and Norway.

294

This picture sign (called a glyph) writes the name Eight Deer, with eight circles and a deer's head.

In ancient Mexico, the Mixtec ruler Eight Deer Jaguar-Claw was a great player of the ball game (see page 115 for more about the ball game). Sometimes the game was used to settle an argument between cities. The winning team would gain control of the city and the losing team would be sacrificed. Eight Deer won several cities in this way, until he finally lost a game, and his life.

Coin of King Cnut, AD 1016–1035.

Powerful women

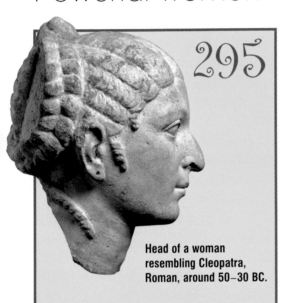

295

Head of a woman resembling Cleopatra, Roman, around 50–30 BC.

Cleopatra VII (reigned 51–30 BC) first ruled Egypt with her half-brother Ptolemy XIII, but he drove her out. Julius Caesar, her Roman lover, helped her regain the throne. She then fought the emperor Augustus, with the help of her second Roman lover, Mark Anthony. She was famous for her charm and cleverness. Augustus finally defeated her in 31 BC. It is often said that Cleopatra poisoned herself with a snake-bite, but this was probably made up by writers in much later times.

296

Empress Irene: when Constantine VI became emperor of Byzantium in AD 780 he was still a child and his mother Irene ruled for him. When he became an adult, she did not want to give up power, and they quarrelled. In 797 Irene had Constantine blinded and imprisoned so he would not be able to rule. Constantine died from his injuries. She then became empress, the first woman to rule Byzantium in her own name.

297

Livia (58 BC–AD 29) was married to Augustus, the first Roman emperor, for over fifty years. Although she had no official position, she had huge power behind the throne. She was still very powerful even after Augustus died. It was rumoured that Livia had several people murdered, including Augustus himself, and his nephew and grandsons. She wanted them out of the way so that her own son Tiberius (by her first marriage) could become the next emperor.

Wu Zetian.

298

Boudica was the ruler of the Iceni tribe in Iron Age Britain. After her husband was killed, she was very harshly treated by the Romans. She led her people in revolt against the Roman invaders. She was eventually defeated and killed in around AD 60 or 61, but first she managed to inflict great damage, destroying Camulodunum (Colchester), Londinium (London) and Verulamium (St Albans) and killing thousands.

299

Of all the hundreds of rulers of ancient Egypt there were only three female rulers who governed in their own right without being married to a king or pharaoh – Queens Sobekneferu, Hatshepsut, and Tawosret.

Gold ring with Hatshepsut's name in hieroglyphs.

300

Wu Zetian (AD 625–705) was the only woman to govern China in her own right in the 2,100-year history of China's emperors. She used the name Shengshen. At first she was a concubine of the emperor, and she used her beauty, cleverness and cruelty to be made empress consort. She had the previous consort put to death horribly by having her arms and legs broken, then leaving her in a huge wine jar for several days. Eventually, when the emperor became ill, she ruled in his place.

Society

How different peoples were ruled

Aztecs

301

The Aztec emperor was completely in charge. He had groups of nobles to advise him. Ordinary people had to do as they were told.

302

The Aztecs actually called themselves the Mexica, which is where the modern name for Mexico comes from. 'Aztec' is a name that was invented for them later.

ROME

303

The emperor held most of the power in ancient Rome. He was advised by the senate, which was a parliament voted in by the Roman citizens. Citizens had to be men born in Rome – women, foreigners and very poor people could not be citizens.

304

There were three classes of Roman citizens. It was possible to move from one class to another if you had enough money. The classes were:

PLEBEIANS (ordinary working men)

EQUITES ('knights' – fairly wealthy men but not nobles)

PATRICIANS (the aristocrats)

Roman emperors wore wreaths of laurel leaves on their heads instead of crowns. This was because they didn't want to be seen as kings, but as military leaders.

Gold oak wreath, 350–300 BC.

305

306

Kings had made themselves pretty unpopular in Rome! Tarquinius Superbus, the last king of Rome, was an arrogant tyrant. The Romans threw him out in 510 BC, and for centuries ruled themselves as a republic instead.

307

After the emperor, the most important men in Rome were the two powerful consuls, in charge of the army and the government.

GREECE

Silver coin showing the goddess Athena and her owl from Athens, around 480 BC.

308

Greece consisted of many different city states and areas, each of which was ruled in its own way. Athens was unusual in that it became a democracy (*demos* means 'people' and *kratos* means 'rule') where citizens who attended the Assembly all had a vote in the running of the city. Women, foreigners and many others were not allowed to vote.

309 Egypt

The pharaoh had a council of specially chosen men to give him advice. The Egyptians believed that the pharaoh was part-divine, and acted a link between the world of men and the gods. So his commands had to be obeyed like those of a god.

CRIME AND PUNISHMENT

310

Being sent to work in the mines was the punishment for many crimes in ancient Egypt. Other punishments included moving large blocks of stone or doing other manual labour. The Egyptians did not punish too harshly on the whole, although stealing from a royal grave got the death penalty.

311

There were police in ancient Egypt but they mainly looked after the pharaoh or king. They didn't help the public at all.

312

The worst punishment in ancient China – for example, for someone who had murdered his or her parents – was to be killed by being slowly cut to pieces.

313

The Roman emperor Diocletian (ruled AD 284–305) thought Christianity was a threat to Roman society. He arrested Christians and sent them to fight wild lions in the arenas without any means of protecting themselves.

Coin of Diocletian, early 4th century AD.

314

In medieval England, the worst crime was treason (plotting against the king). The punishment was hanging, drawing and quartering. First the victim would be dragged to the place of execution then hanged until not quite dead, then drawn (disembowelled) and their body parts burned in front of them. Then the victim was cut into four quarters, which would be displayed in different cities around the country to put other people off committing the same crime.

315

When they reached the age of about thirteen, Spartan boys were tested by being sent out into the countryside where they had to steal in order to survive. However, if they got caught they were severely beaten.

316

Roman slaves were punished very harshly if they tried to run away. They could be burned alive or sent to the arena to be killed by wild beasts.

Metal tag which was probably attached to a slave – or a dog. The writing says ' Hold me if I run away and return me to my master Viventius on the estate of Callistus'.

Women

317

According to Confucian custom in ancient China, men made the rules and women were supposed to obey them. A woman had to do what her parents told her, then what her husband told her, and when he died what her eldest son told her. However, in practice some women had great power over their children.

Chinese family in a garden, 18th century AD.

318

At special occasions, such as dinner parties, Greek women were not allowed to eat with the men but stayed in their own quarters. However, paid female entertainers might eat with the men.

319

Roman women could not vote or hold powerful office. The only job in which they could achieve rank was as a priestess. All other important posts were open to men only.

320

Greek actors were all men. Women were probably not even allowed to watch plays.

Marble bust of a Roman lady, made around AD 40–50.

321

It was legal in ancient Greece to leave female babies outside to die, if their parents could not afford to keep them.

322

A woman's place in ancient Egypt was in the home. Women's skin is often coloured paler than men's in wall paintings to show that they spent most of their time indoors.

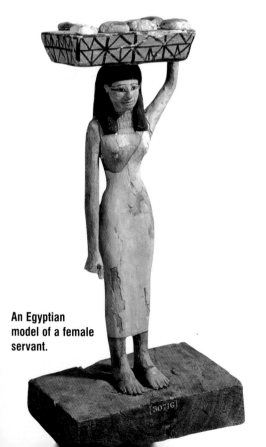

An Egyptian model of a female servant.

97

The spiritual world

Religion

Pagans are people who worship a number of gods, often gods of nature. Most people in Europe were pagan before the coming of Christianity. Christians believe in one God. Christianity spread rapidly across Europe from late Roman and early medieval times, although many people did not abandon their pagan gods quickly or without resistance.

323

Six people in Christian prayer. They were painted on the wall of a Roman villa in eastern Britain.

324

King Oswald of Northumbria (AD 633–42) was an early Anglo-Saxon Christian king who was killed in battle by the pagan king Penda of Mercia. His head and limbs were impaled on spikes. Oswald was made into a saint and one description of his head says it was '... glowing a deep yellow colour which surpasses the yellowness of wax and is closer in its great beauty and loveliness to the appearance of gold ...'

325

The Vikings were pagans. Odin was the chief of their gods. He carried a spear and had one eye. He had two ravens called Huginn and Muninn (thought and memory) who whispered secrets to him.

326

The Druids were important priests who carried out religious rituals in the Iron Age in Britain. They may have sacrificed humans. Mistletoe pollen was found in the stomach of Lindow Man (see page 14) and this plant was important to Druids.

327

In Bronze Age and Iron Age Britain, many weapons were thrown into water or buried in the ground, perhaps as sacrifices (gifts) to the pagan gods. This has helped preserve the weapons for us to study.

This shield was thrown into the River Thames, London, England between 350 and 50 BC.

328

Reliquaries are containers which hold the relics of saints, such as their teeth, finger-bones or hair. They have been used by many religions. This silver reliquary was made in the shape of a head to keep pieces from the skull of the Christian saint, Eustace. According to legend Eustace was a Roman general who converted to Christianity and was burned to death with his family when he refused to give thanks to the Roman gods.

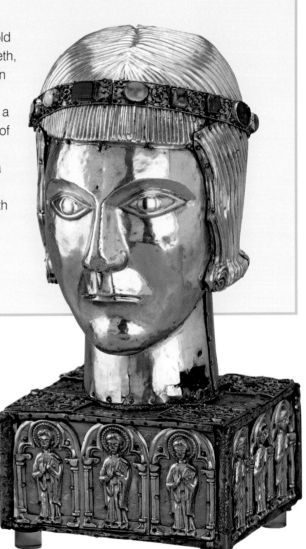

Reliquary of St Eustace, AD 1210.

329 TWELVE GREEK GODS

The Greeks believed that their twelve main gods lived at the top of high Mount Olympus, in north-east Greece. They were:

Zeus — king of the gods and god of the weather

Poseidon — god of the sea

Hera — wife of Zeus, goddess of marriage and of the sky and stars

Demeter — the goddess of farming and the earth

Hestia — goddess of home and family

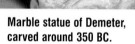

These first five were brothers and sisters. The other seven Olympian gods were children of Zeus:

Marble statue of Demeter, carved around 350 BC.

Artemis — goddess of animals and the hunt and protector of young girls

Apollo — god of light, telling the future, music, medicine and archery

Athena — goddess of wisdom, crafts, education and war. Her symbol was the owl.

Hephaestus — the craftsman of the gods, also the god of fire, workmen and weapons

Ares — the god of war and slaughter

Aphrodite — the goddess of love and beauty

Hermes — the messenger of the gods, and also the god of travellers, trade and inventions

Bronze head of Apollo, from around 460 BC.

330

Hades was the next most powerful Greek god after Zeus and Poseidon, but he ruled over the underworld, and so he did not live on Mount Olympus.

331

Ordinary people weren't allowed inside sacred Greek temples, so the altars were put outside where they could worship.

332

Dionysus was the Greek god of wine, plants and the theatre. He is not always considered to be an Olympian because his mother was a mortal (a human who would die, and therefore not a god).

ROMAN GODS

333

The Romans had many different gods and goddesses ruled by Jupiter, the god of thunder and the sky. Their most important gods were shared with ancient Greece and given Roman names (such as Bacchus instead of Dionysus), and the Romans also worshipped extra gods from peoples they had conquered.

Bronze figure of Jupiter, 2nd century AD. He probably once held a thunderbolt.

334

The Romans, like many other ancient peoples, believed that blood sacrifices (killing an animal) were the best way to talk to the gods. On her birthday, a Roman woman would sacrifice an animal as a present to the goddess Juno, queen of the gods. White animals, such as sheep, were often sacrificed to Jupiter, as his special colour was white.

335

The Romans held many festivals to honour the gods. They had thirty-two festivals just in the month of January.

336

The Vestal Virgins were women who worked in the temple for the goddess Vesta in Rome, keeping the sacred fire always burning for her. Vesta was the Roman name for Hestia, Greek goddess of the hearth.

337

Roman priests and priestesses covered their heads with a veil, or a fold of the toga, when they performed sacrifices to the gods.

338

Roman figure of Bacchus holding an empty wine-cup, with his panther at his feet.

In places the riotous worship of the wine-god Bacchus got really out of hand. The Romans tried to ban it altogether, but in the end they were forced to control it and bring it more into mainstream religion.

The ancient Egyptians worshipped many gods. Most of these gods had animals associated with them, and could be shown with animal heads.

339 SIX EGYPTIAN ANIMAL-HEADED GODS

1 **ANUBIS**, with the head of a jackal, mummified and protected the dead.
2 **RE**, the powerful sun god, had the head of a falcon.
3 **THOTH**, with the head of an ibis (a kind of bird) or a baboon, was the scribe of the gods.
4 **HATHOR**, the daughter of Re and goddess of music and dancing, had the head of a cow.
5 **SEKHMET**, a goddess who was a ferocious protector of Re, had the head of a lioness.
6 **KHEPRI**, with the head of a scarab beetle, was said to push the sun through the sky.

Statue of Sekhmet.

Statue of a baboon from Egypt, 1350 BC.

Anubis supervising the 'Weighing of the Heart' ceremony, to judge if a dead person had been good or bad.

340

In ancient Egypt each god had many temples. In the main temples, the king and high priests performed certain rites and received offerings. Ordinary people were never allowed inside a temple. They only saw a god's statue during special festivals when it was carried outside the temple in a procession.

341 SEVEN ATZEC GODS

The Aztecs believed in a huge number of gods who created and controlled the world, and kept the sun moving across the sky.

1 **Quetzalcoatl**, 'Feathered serpent', was the god of learning and of the wind.
2 **Tezcatlipoca**, 'Smoking mirror', was the god of night, sorcery and war. He was twinned with Quetzalcoatl, whose opposite he was.
3 **Xipe Totec**, 'Our flayed lord', was the god of the seasons, growth and vegetation. He is usually shown wearing a flayed (stripped) human skin.
4 **Tlaloc**, the great provider, god of fertility and rain.
5 **Coatlicue**, 'She of the serpent skirt', mother of the moon and stars and goddess of women who die in childbirth.
6 **Chicomecoatl**, the goddess of ripe maize. The Aztecs had three goddesses just for the maize plant (sweetcorn), their most important crop.
7 **Chalchiuhtlicue** was the goddess of the waters, and wore a skirt the colour of water.

Mosaic mask of Tezcatlipoca, based on a human skull. 15th–16th century AD.

342

The ancient Maya believed that in shedding their own blood they were making contact with the gods and showing that they were brave. One Maya carving shows a queen passing a rope of thorns through her tongue and another shows her husband pricking his penis with a sharp stick.

343

The Maya believed that the gods watched everything they did, and it was important to perform the right rituals every day to keep the gods happy. They had many gods and goddesses – of the stars and the sun, of rain, of maize and of different months and days.

Maya carving from Yaxchilan, Mexico, showing the queen shedding her blood.

344

In ancient China several different belief systems existed side by side. They included Buddhism, Daoism and Confucianism. Confucius (Kong Fu zi, the master Kong, 551–479 BC) was a Chinese philosopher who said that people should honour their families and ancestors, and that this would eventually strengthen the whole country. Today there are still many belief systems in China.

A rubbing of Confucius.

345

Muslims, Christians and Jews all believe in only one God. All three religions look to Abraham as a respected forefather. In the Muslim holy book, the Qur'an, Christians, Jews and Muslims are called 'the Children of the Book'.

The beginning of the *basmala*, which starts every chapter of the Qur'an, 'In the name of Allah the merciful …'

346

Hinduism probably comes from a much older religion found in the ancient Indus Valley in India over 4,000 years ago. Hinduism as a religion did not start until hundreds of years after the Indus Valley civilization died out, and the connection between the two remains a mystery.

347

The sacred books of Hinduism are called the Vedas. There are four Vedas. They are a collection of truths revealed by the gods. They were written down before 1000 BC and are the only surviving records from this time. The first book is the holiest. It is called the Rig Veda.

348 THE THREE MOST IMPORTANT HINDU GODS

Since about 100 BC, the three most important Hindu gods have been:

1 **Brahma**, 'The Creator', a four-headed god whose fifth head was cut off by Shiva.

2 **Vishnu**, 'The Preserver', has appeared in a number of incarnations in order to help mankind. Hindus say that his latest appearance was as Buddha in the sixth century AD.

3 **Shiva**, 'The Destroyer', the most powerful god of all, who can appear in various forms. His consort is the goddess Parvati.

349

The *Mahabharata* and the *Ramayana* are the two great epic poems of ancient India. They are very important to the Hindu religion. The *Mahabharata* is a collection of myths about the main Hindu gods, and the *Ramayana* is the story of Rama and Sita. It is hard to date these, but a first version of the *Ramayana* was probably written around 500–300 BC, while the *Mahabharata* was written in the second century AD.

Statuette of Parvati, the wife of Shiva. From India, early 11th century AD.

350

Gautama Siddhartha was born in India in about 560 BC. He was a royal prince whose family kept him hidden away in the palace. When he was nearly thirty he finally sneaked out and discovered to his horror that people could suffer and die. He decided to stop being a prince and travel the land looking for happiness and freedom from these worries. He finally achieved this and people started called him Buddha, which means 'the enlightened'. He spent the rest of his life teaching and helping others. The religion of Buddhism is named after him.

Carving of the feet of the Buddha from Amaravati, India, 1st century BC.

Foretelling the future

351

The Aztecs used mirrors of obsidian (black volcanic glass) to help them foresee the future. For example, if a son or daughter was sick, parents would look at the child's reflection in the mirror. If it was clear, the child would get better, but if it was shadowy, the soul was lost and the child would die.

Aztec obsidian mirror from Mexico, AD 1325–1521.

352

The ancient Greeks believed in fate. In other words, your future was already mapped out for you and you couldn't change it. The Greeks visited places called oracles, where their futures could be foretold. The oracle at Delphi was the most famous. Here, after the sacrifice of a goat, the main priestess (the Pythia) would tell people their fate. According to some accounts she first inhaled some vapours rising from the ground which made her speak in a strange voice.

353

The *Y Jing* (Book of Changes) is the most ancient of Chinese texts. It gives advice for life based on cosmology and philosophy and provides a system for explaining chance events. In ancient China the sixty-four hexagons of the Y Jing were used to tell people's fortunes. Sticks, such as yarrow stalks, were thrown. The pattern they made when they fell was matched to a hexagram diagram, and the symbol was then interpreted.

Magic and curses

354

On the back of this beautiful silver Anglo-Saxon brooch is inscribed: 'Ædwen owns me, may the Lord own her. May the Lord curse him who takes me from her, unless she gives me of her own free will'.

355

Amulets are small objects that are worn or carried for good luck and protection against harm. Most cultures have used them, including the Egyptians, Romans and Anglo-Saxons. The ancient Egyptians sometimes strung several on to jewellery, like this ancient version of a modern charm bracelet.

Egyptian amulet bracelet.

356

Archaeologists found a piece of lead from Roman Britain with these words scratched on it: 'I curse Tretia Maria and her life and mind and memory and liver and lungs mixed up together, and her words, thoughts and memory'.

357

This Egyptian wax figure was used to cast a spell on a person. It has a scroll in its back with the spell written on it, and human hair pushed into its navel. Spells were used in ancient Egypt by priests and doctors, as well as ordinary people. The Egyptians were particularly worried that something might happen to them while they were asleep. Children would be given written spells to protect them from harm, such as being buried by a falling house, or getting worms.

Sport

358

Gladiators were men (and occasionally women) who had to fight, sometimes to the death, in Roman arenas. They battled against wild beasts and each other, purely for the pleasure of the onlookers.

Bronze figurine of a gladiator, 1st–2nd century AD.

EIGHT FACTS
ABOUT GLADIATORS

359 For over 650 years, gladiatorial fights were held across the Roman empire. Thousands of gladiators were killed.

360 Under the empire people came to expect magnificent spectacles. One show given by the emperor Trajan lasted for 117 days, with nearly 5,000 pairs of gladiators.

361 Gladiators were usually slaves and had no choice whether they fought or not.

362 At the end of a fight, the emperor would decide whether the gladiator's life should be spared by turning his thumb outwards for all to see.

363 At the first fight ever held in the Colosseum in Rome, 5,000 animals were killed.

364 The Colosseum was such a big arena that 60,000 people could fit into it to watch gladiator fights.

365 The emperor Septimius Severus banned female gladiators in AD 200.

366 Eventually the cost in lives and money together with objections from the Christian church led to the contests being abolished in about AD 400.

367 TEN TYPES OF ROMAN GLADIATOR AND THEIR KIT

Retiarius (net and trident)
Secutor (short sword and long shield)
Murmillo (heavy armour and crested helmet)
Hoplomachus (spear and small round shield)
Thraex (curved sword and square shield)
Provocator (helmet with visor, sword and large shield)
Eques (on horseback)
Essedarius (chariots)
Crupellarius (so heavily armed that if he fell over he couldn't get up again)
Venator (fought wild animals)

Murmillo's helmet, said to be from Pompeii, Italy. 1st century AD.

368 TEN 'STAGE NAMES' OF ROMAN GLADIATORS

A secutor.

Amethystus (amethyst)
Margarites (pearl)
Beryllus (beryl)
Smaragdus (emerald)
Leo (lion)
Ferox (ferocious)
Triumphus (the winner)
Tigris (tiger)
Invictus (unbeaten)
Rapidus (swift)

A murmillo.

113

369

The Vikings made ice-skates from the leg-bones of cows and horses. They didn't skate just for fun – it made travel easier in winter, when the lakes and rivers froze.

371

The game of lacrosse was first played by the Iroquois, a North American people. It was introduced from Canada into Europe in the middle of the nineteenth century.

370

The Romans loved watching chariot races. Every major city had a stadium, where the races were held. The largest stadium by far was the Circus Maximus in Rome, which could hold 250,000 people. The winners of important races could become very wealthy celebrities, and the very passionate supporters of the various racing teams often ended up fighting each other. In Rome, the racing teams were the reds, whites, greens and blues.

Model of a Roman two-horse racing chariot (*biga*), 1st–2nd century AD.

Pair of Creek ballsticks from Oklahoma, North America, around 1977.

372

Stickball is a North American game played by the Creek people, who lived in the Alabama and Georgia regions in the eighteenth and nineteenth centuries. Each player held two long wooden sticks with leather nets at the end. A deerskin ball stuffed with hair was thrown and caught in the net. Two towns would play each other – the goals were 400 metres (437 yards) apart, and each side had sixty-two players.

373

The word gymnasium comes from the Greek word gymnos, which means 'naked', because Greek athletes competed naked.

374

The ancient Maya and Aztec ball-game was a religious event, not just a sport. It was fast-paced and exciting, played on a special enclosed court. Two teams tried to keep the ball in the air, but were only allowed to use their elbows, hips or knees to hit it. Players wore special protective clothing. You didn't want to be on the losing team, as occasionally they could be sacrificed.

The Aztec ball-game.

EIGHT EVENTS
of the ancient Olympic games

375

1 Chariot races
2 Horse races
3 Pentathlon (discus, javelin, jumping, running, wrestling)
4 Running
5 Wrestling
6 Boxing
7 *Pankration* (see fact 383 in the Top Ten facts about the Olympic Games, opposite)
8 *Hoplitodromia* (see fact 381)

The *hoplitodromia*.

Amphora with runners.

Discus-thrower.

Horse race.

Wrestlers.

Boxers.

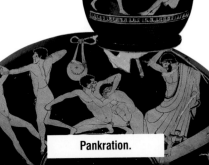

Pankration.

TOP TEN FACTS
ABOUT THE OLYMPIC GAMES

376 Before the games began the athletes, their trainers and their fathers had to swear to Zeus that they had trained for ten months and that they would obey the rules.

377 If two neighbouring Greek states were at war, they called a truce (stopped fighting) during the Olympic Games so that their athletes could travel safely.

378 Chariot racing could be very dangerous. Once, forty chariots entered an Olympic race and only one finished it. The rest crashed.

379 Olympic wrestlers wore tight-fitting caps so that their opponents could not pull their hair.

380 The marathon was not run in ancient Greece. It was actually invented in 1876, for the first modern Olympic Games.

381 The *hoplitodromia* was a race in which men had to run in full armour under the baking sun.

382 There was also the mule-cart race, which was only included for fourteen Olympic games because of an ancient curse on mules bred within the sacred area of Olympia.

383 The *pankration* was a cross between boxing and wrestling. Any attack was allowed except for biting or gouging out your opponent's eyes.

384 The greatest victory for an athlete was to win the Olympic crown, the prize for each event winner. The crown was a wreath of wild olive cut from the tree sacred to Zeus.

385 Number of women allowed to attend Olympic games: one, the priestess of Demeter. One writer said that any other women discovered at the games would be thrown off a cliff! Women had their own event at Olympia called the Heraia, which included only running races.

Model of ancient Olympia. The white building in the middle is the temple of Zeus.

Towns and buildings

Towns

Ostrich egg cup from the ancient city of Ur, 2600–2200 BC.

386

The very first cities in the world included Ur, Eridu and Nippur. They were built by the ancient Sumerians, who lived in Mesopotamia (now Iraq) over 4,000 years ago. No one knew that the ancient Sumerians even existed until about 100 years ago.

387

Babylon in Mesopotamia was the capital city of King Nebuchadnezzar II, in the sixth century BC. It had two lots of huge walls and massive palaces and temples, including a towering central ziggurat (a temple building in the shape of a stepped pyramid). It is said that at this time Nebuchadnezzar built the famous 'hanging gardens of Babylon' (see page 126).

388

Roman towns seemed very sophisticated to the people they conquered. The towns were specially planned by architects to be like Rome, and included:

basilicas (large meeting halls)
bathhouses
town halls
theatres
amphitheatres.

389

The centre of any Roman town was the forum, a large open area used for markets, sport and meetings. Around the forum were the main government buildings and the temple.

The temple of Saturn in the forum at Rome (painting by Francis Towne).

390

Roman towns included large public toilets. These had several spaces for men, women and children to sit down together in the same room. Sometimes marble toilet seats were set over channels where flowing water made the first flush toilets. A shallow water channel in front of the seats held sponges attached to sticks for patrons to wipe themselves.

391

Most of the very poor in the city of Rome lived in dangerously run-down apartment blocks called *insulae*. These could be four or five floors high.

392

The government gave out free food handouts in Rome to the very poor. By the year 2 BC, about 200,000 people were registered for these handouts.

393

During the reign of the emperor Nero, a huge fire raged through the crowded wooden apartment blocks of Rome. Many of Nero's subjects were made homeless by the fire. Nero did not help them, but built himself a sumptuous palace called the Golden House shortly afterwards. This made Nero very unpopular and the tale spread that Nero had started the fire, then sung poetry while watching the flames.

395

On ancient Chinese streets pedestrians had to give way to people carrying loads, who had to give way to empty sedan chairs, who had to give way to people in sedan chairs, who had to give way to horses. Everyone had to give way to important officials or wedding parties. Because it was polite to get down from your sedan chair or horse to greet a friend, sometimes pedestrians would hide their faces with fans to save their friends the trouble.

394

When the people of the town of Pompeii looked up into the sky on the morning of 24 August in the year AD 79, they saw 'a cloud rising in shape rather like a pine tree' over the volcano Vesuvius. This was the start of the eruption that was to kill hundreds of people, burying the town under four metres (thirteen feet) of rubble and ash.

Wall painting from a house in Pompeii showing Odysseus and the Sirens.

396 SIX PIECES OF
ROMAN GRAFFITI FROM POMPEII

1. Jarinus, you live here (*in the bathhouse*)
2. Celadus the Thraex makes the girls sigh!
   (*in the barracks of the gladiators*)
3. Profit is happiness!
4. I've caught a cold
5. Epaphra, you are bald!
6. O walls, you have held up so much tedious graffiti that I am
   amazed that you have not already collapsed in ruin

397

From about 2600 BC to 1700 BC many towns and cities were built on and around the banks of the River Indus in north-west India. These settlements covered a huge region, twice as large as ancient Egypt. The cities of the Indus Valley were solidly built out of brick and stone. They had streets planned on a grid system. Houses had two floors, and each house had its own bathing area with a drain emptying into the city's main drainage system.

Seal from the city of Harappa in the Indus Valley, 2600–1900 BC.

398 SIX ANGLO-SAXON
place name endings

1	**-burh** (modern *-burgh*)	fort, later also fortified town
2	**-dun/down/den**	down (hill)
3	**-ham**	village
4	**-wic**	settlement, later a trading settlement
5	**-tun** (Modern *-ton*)	settlement
6	**-ford**	river crossing

so:

Deptford	Deep ford
Oxford	Shallow ford where oxen crossed
Fordham	The village by the river crossing
Greenwich	Farm with fields
Woolwich	Farm with sheep

399 EIGHT VIKING
place name endings

1	**-byr** (modern *-by*)	farm or village
2	**-thorp** (modern *-thorpe*)	farm or village
3	**-toft**	homestead
4	**-holmr** (modern *-holme*)	island or reclaimed land
5	**-nes** (modern *-ness*)	headland
6	**-fjell** (modern *-fell*)	mountain
7	**-dalr** (modern *-dale*)	valley
8	**-bekkr** (modern *-beck*)	brook

so:

Grimsby	Grim's village
Lowestoft	Hlothver's homestead
Skegness	Skeggi's headland

400

When Viking and Saxon names became mixed up …

It was bound to happen as the Vikings and the Saxons started to marry each other and settle the land together. Grimston means 'Grim's farm'. Grim is a Viking name, but 'ton' is the Saxon word for 'farm'. Because of this name, mixed Viking and Saxon place names are sometimes called Grimston hybrids. A hybrid is a mixture of two things.

401

The main Viking centre in Britain for around 200 years was Jorvik (modern York). Archaeologists have found many things left behind by the people who lived there, including jewellery, cups, bowls, coins, and even a woollen sock. Viking Jorvik must have been a very smelly place. Rubbish was thrown into open drains in the street.

402

Aztec town life centred on the marketplace, where goods and gossip were exchanged. Aztec marketplaces were huge and bustling. Many different goods were bought and sold, from basic foods like maize to rare imports such as jaguar skins and precious stones.

403

The Aztec capital Tenochtitlan was built on an island in middle of Lake Texcoco with four causeways (raised paths) leading across to it. According to legend their god Huitzilopochtli told them to build the city where they saw an eagle land on a cactus. In the centre of Tenochtitlan was a large square with a large pyramid on which stood the temples of the gods Tlaloc and Huitzilopochtli.

A thousand years old and it still has all its teeth! A Viking comb from Jorvik, 9th–10th century AD.

404

Ordinary people were not allowed into the Forbidden City in China. It was built in AD 1420 to be the centre of government and to house the family of the emperor of China, right in the centre of Beijing. The city of Beijing was built in a grid pattern (like modern American cities), so that people could get around easily. The streets ran from north to south and east to west in order to create good *feng shui*, bringing good luck and energy to the town.

405

Ancient Greece consisted of many different city-states. The two best known were probably Athens and Sparta. They were very different. During the Classical Period, the citizens of Athens had a say in the running of the city (it was a democracy). Sparta focused on producing good soldiers and all Spartan male citizens were part of the army.

Architecture

406

Some Anglo-Saxons lived among the ruins of Roman towns. They decided that giants (whom they called Ents) must have built the huge crumbling remains.

407

The first cities of ancient Mesopotamia were built around huge temples called ziggurats. These were made of brick and had steeply stepped sides.

408

The Maya of Mexico (AD 300–900) also built large cities and temples with stepped sides, steeper even than the ziggurats of Mesopotamia. Maya legend told that the towering Temple of the Magician at Uxmal was built in one night single-handedly by a magician-god named Itzamna.

409

Greek temples are famous for their impressive columns. The portico (the porch with the columns at the front) of the British Museum copies a Greek style of architecture. The tall pillars gradually taper at the top so that they look straight and even when you look up at them.

The front of the British Museum, which is based on the temple of Athena at Priene.

The remains of the ziggurat of Ur.

125

THE SEVEN WONDERS
of the ancient world

410

The Pyramids of Giza, Egypt,
around 2551–2472 BC

The Great Pyramid was built by the
Egyptian king Khufu. It was almost 150 m
(492 ft) high, and used over 2,000,000
stone blocks. The capstone at the top was
coated with gold. To this day, no one
knows exactly how the Egyptians managed
to lift the huge blocks into place.

411

The Hanging Gardens of Babylon
(modern Iraq), 605–562 BC

The most mysterious of the wonders, as
we don't know what they looked like or
how they were watered. Perhaps they were
built on a series of steps, giving a hanging
effect as foliage trailed over the edge of
each level.

412

The Temple of Artemis at Ephesus,
Turkey, around 550–325 BC

Famous because of its huge size –
115 m x 55 m (377 ft x 170 ft) – and its
many decorated pillars, but also because
it contained a vast statue of the goddess
Artemis made from gold, silver, ebony
and black stone.

413

The Statue of Zeus at Olympia, Greece, around 430 BC

This masterpiece stood in the temple of Zeus at Olympia. It was around 12 m (39 ft) high, plated with gold and ivory. It showed the god sitting on a decorated throne with his hands outstretched.

414

The Colossus of Rhodes, Greece, 294–282 BC

This was a huge – 32 m (105 ft) high – bronze statue of the sun god Helios, put up by the harbour in the city of Rhodes to commemorate the end of a long siege.

415

The Mausoleum of Halicarnassus, (modern Bodrum, Turkey), around 353 BC

This huge tomb was built for King Mausollos by his widow Artemisia. Our word for a large tomb – mausoleum – is taken from his name. It included thirty-six marble columns and a stepped roof topped with a huge marble chariot pulled by four horses.

Statue from the Mausoleum, probably Mausollos.

416

The Pharos (Lighthouse) of Alexandria, Egypt, 297–283 BC

The lighthouse stood on the island of Pharos in the harbour at Alexandria. It was 110 m (351 ft) high. Only the Great Pyramid of Giza was taller in the ancient world.

Fragment of a column from the Temple of Artemis.

Houses

417

The poorest Romans lived in one- or two-room apartments. Essential services such as fires for cooking and water for washing were provided outside, and were shared by a number of families.

418

Many rich Romans had villas, country houses where they lived for all or part of the year. Some villas had fine gardens with pools and fountains, others were working farms with bakeries and oil presses.

419

Roman houses had central heating. This came from a hypocaust. Slaves stoked a fire in the cellar, and the hot air from this would flow up through spaces underneath the floor of the house. Central heating from hypocausts was especially used in the colder northern provinces of the empire, such as Germany and Britain.

420

Greek houses were built around courtyards. Many family activities, such as food preparation and cooking, took place in the courtyard, especially in summer. Inside the house, the floors were earth beaten flat. There was very little furniture and the windows were small. There was no heating except for the central fire, used for cooking, and oil lamps provided only a little light.

421

Aztec houses were made of earth and straw bricks called adobe. They were built around courtyards. The Aztecs used chairs and sleeping-mats made from reeds.

422

The floors and walls of houses owned by wealthy Romans were decorated with paintings and mosaics, pictures made from tiny pieces of tile called tesserae. These mosaics often had a central picture surrounded by patterns. The Leadenhall Street mosaic shows Bacchus riding on a tiger.

Leadenhall Street Mosaic from London, Britain, 1st or 2nd century AD.

Painting of a garden pool, from the tomb-chapel of a man called Nebamun, around 1350 BC.

423

Houses in ancient Egypt were built of mud-brick, which was plastered and whitewashed to reflect the sun. The houses had tiny windows to keep them cool. The houses did not have much furniture, but there were benches to eat and sleep on. When it was very hot, people sometimes slept on the flat roof.

Model of a house from Egypt, about 1900 BC.

424

Shady gardens made a welcome retreat from the hot sun in ancient Egypt, but only the richest Egyptians could afford them. Here they grew vegetables, flowers and grapes, and had ponds filled with fish and water-lilies. Temples had the biggest gardens, so that they could grow all the flowers and plants needed for offerings to the gods.

War

The Roman army

425

A century: a Roman centurion was in charge of eighty men (not a hundred, despite the name).

426

A legion: the number of soldiers in a Roman legion = 5,000. The legions were the backbone of the Roman army. They were heavily-armed and strictly disciplined. A young man would sign up aged around eighteen for about twenty-five years' service. In return, he got good pay, and he would be granted Roman citizenship and given money or land when he retired.

Bronze statue of a Roman legionary, 2nd century AD.

427

Auxiliaries: auxiliaries were non-Roman citizens recruited from conquered countries. Auxiliaries often had military skills that the legionary soldiers didn't. They might be expert archers, sling-shot men, or cavalry. They did not get paid as much as legionaries but when they retired they were granted citizenship.

428

Equipment: Even on a 30 km (18 mile) training march a Roman legionary would carry a huge amount of equipment. This included:

SWORD	TURF-CUTTER
DAGGER	PAN
SHIELD	DISH
KNIFE	CHAIN
SAW	CLOAK
BASKET	FOOD AND DRINK
AXE	FOR THREE DAYS.

Iron sword, made in the first century AD.

Roman cavalrymen.

429

Roman soldiers on the march drank vinegar. This wasn't as nasty as it sounds. It was actually cheap wine blended with water into a refreshing drink called *posca*.

430

The Roman emperor Claudius used elephants in the invasion of Britain. They must have terrified the native Britons, and were used successfully in the conquest of Camulodunum (Colchester).

431

In the Greek city-state of Sparta, fighting was taken extremely seriously. Having joined the army at the age of seven, all boys and young men lived in barracks until they were thirty years old. Even if they got married, they could only visit their wives in secret.

433

'Viking' means 'pirate'. The Vikings earned this name by raiding and fighting abroad. At home the Vikings were farmers, but they discovered that piracy could be a more profitable career. They attacked their near neighbours, Britain and Europe. Later, though, Vikings went on to settle as farmers in Iceland, Greenland, and even North America.

432

The foot-soldiers called *hoplites* were the most important part of a Greek army during the later part of ancient Greek history. Hoplites carried a bronze shield and iron weapons and were protected by armour. Some threw short spears at the enemy, and some fought with long thrusting spears.

Greek soldiers fighting with spears and shields.

Hoplite's helmet from Greece, 460 BC.

434

The first Viking raid on Britain was in AD 793, when they attacked the rich monastery of Lindisfarne, unprotected on its island in the north-east of England. A priest wrote: 'Never before has such a terror come to Britain as this … nor was it thought possible that such an invasion could come from the sea'.

436

Samurai armour. These pieces of armour were made between the 16th and 19th centuries AD and include a metal breastplate, to stop bullets!

435

In Aztec Mexico one of the top jobs a man could do was to become a warrior. The two top groups of noble warriors were called the jaguars and the eagles. To join one of these groups a warrior had to take more than four prisoners in battle.

An Aztec eagle warrior, AD 1325–1521.

The first samurai warriors in Japan fought for the emperor in the eighth century AD. Gradually they gained power for themselves, and in 1192 the first samurai emperor took control. The samurai were highly-trained fighters, usually Zen Buddhists, who lived very simply and with great self-control.

Weapons and armour

437

Celtic men from western Europe from around 700 BC would rush into battle shouting. They made themselves look more frightening by combing lime into their hair so that it stuck up in spikes. They also painted patterns on their skins with a blue dye made from the woad plant. It must have been terrifying to see them charging at you.

438

Greek fire was a substance which would burn fiercely in air and on water. It would even burn under water, and it could not be put out. Greek fire was first used by the Byzantines in a sea battle in AD 673. Nobody knows what it was made from. One ingredient may have been naptha, a crude form of petrol.

Sword from the ship burial at Sutton Hoo, early 7th century AD.

439

As a Spartan man went off to war his wife would give him his shield, saying that he should return 'with this or upon it'. If he came back with his shield, he was alive and safe. If he came back on his shield he was dead, and was being carried home in honour by other soldiers. If he came back without his shield it would be assumed that he had run away from battle, and he would be banished or even executed.

440

The weapon most commonly used by Anglo-Saxon warriors was the spear.

441

Few Anglo-Saxon warriors could afford swords. They were often passed down from father to son, or sometimes buried with their owner when he died. Swords could be given names.

442

The first Europeans to reach West Africa were the Portuguese, who arrived in the kingdom of Benin (now Nigeria) between AD 1482 and 1496. They introduced guns to the Africans and became rich trading with them.

Model of a Portuguese soldier holding a gun from Benin, 17th century AD.

443

Japanese sword-makers were very skilled. They made fine blades by folding and hammering, then heating the metal and plunging it into cold water. This meant that the blade was strong but sharp enough to cut through armour. A samurai warrior's sword was so important to him that there are many different words in Japanese just for the different parts of a sword: the pattern on the edge of the blade, the fine point, the curve towards the hilt and so on.

444

Gunpowder was invented in China in the second to third centuries, probably as a by-product of alchemist's experiments. The Chinese first used gunpowder in warfare in AD 904. By 1132 it was used to fire projectiles, such as arrows, from bamboo tubes. The explosive power of the gunpowder when it was lit hurled the missiles very effectively at the enemy.

Sieges

445

In AD 71 the Romans besieged the city of Jerusalem. The siege ended when the Romans set fire to the Temple. They probably killed tens of thousands of people. Most of the dead were Jews who had gathered to celebrate the Passover.

Scene from the Nereid monument showing Greek soldiers attacking a city wall, 390–380 BC.

446

Genghis Khan and other Mongol rulers were very successful at besieging cities. One tactic was to use catapults to launch the corpses of plague victims over the walls. These would quickly spread disease – an early form of biological warfare.

448

Ladders with wheels are the first known siege weapons. They are shown on ancient Egyptian tomb carvings from as early as 2400 BC. The Egyptians used them to attack Canaanite towns.

447

The story of the Trojan War tells how after a ten-year siege the city of Troy was finally captured by the Greeks. They hid their best warriors inside a huge wooden horse, left it outside the city gates, then pretended to sail away. The Trojans believed that it would bring them luck if they offered the horse to the goddess Athena, and broke down their walls to get it into the city. While they feasted, the warriors inside the horse sprang out, and the Greeks took the Trojans by surprise.

A model wooden horse greets visitors at Troy today.

449

Alexander the Great conducted many successful sieges. The Phoenician city of Tyre was heavily fortified and built on an island 1 km (1,093 yds) off the coast. It was considered impossible to defeat. Alexander built a wide causeway out to the island, then attacked the walls with catapults and stone throwers. Tyre still managed to hold out for seven months before surrendering in 332 BC.

450

The ancient Assyrians were skilled in war, and wall carvings from their palaces show sieges in progress. Their battering rams were sophisticated, and they even had something like early tanks. These were wooden engines on wheels, and from the tops archers could shoot over city walls.

Assyrians punishing prisoners (probably flaying them alive) at the siege of Lachish, 701 BC.

SEVEN ANCIENT
SIEGE WEAPONS

451 **Battering ram**: used to break down gates and walls. Could have a protective roof and contain archers or other soldiers.

452 **Catapult**: could fire anything, from stones and bundles of wood that had been set on fire to corpses. The Roman onager catapult was named after a wild ass because of its kicking power.

453 **Flamethrower**: these threw out a long stream of fire. The flames could have come from a mysterious concoction called Greek fire.

454 **Siege tower**: a tall tower, usually with wheels, which attackers would push up to the walls.

455 **Trebuchet**: much more accurate than catapults, these could fire missiles over long distances or batter walls.

456 **Agger**: Roman earthen ramp, built to scale walls.

457 **Ballista**: powerful crossbow first developed in ancient Greece.

458

Demetrius I of Macedon invented an incredible siege machine called *helepolis* ('taker of cities'), which was plated with iron and stood nine stories (40 m, or 131 ft) high. He used this to conquer Rhodes in 305–304 BC.

Some famous military campaigns

459

Hannibal was one of the few commanders to oppose the power of Rome successfully. He gathered together an army – famously including elephants – and marched from Spain through southern France and over the mountains into northern Italy. Here he won many battles. However, he never had enough power to attack Rome itself and his campaign was eventually defeated. He was fantastic at war tactics, and the Romans even adopted some of his ideas themselves. Hannibal was a general of Carthage, a city on the coast of North Africa (Tunisia).

A coin from Carthage showing Hannibal on an elephant, 230 BC.

460

Each Greek city-state had its own army, and these often fought against each other. The Peloponnesian War, between Athens and Sparta, lasted for twenty-seven years from 431 BC until 404 BC. The Spartans won by laying siege to Athens, then breaking in when the city was weakened by the plague.

461

The Aztec Conquest

Hernán Cortès of Spain landed on the eastern shore of Mexico in AD 1519 with around 600 men, 17 horses and 10 cannon. Realising that he was hugely outnumbered, he burned most of his fleet of ships so that his soldiers could not desert. He made allies of the Tlaxcalans, who were enemies of the Aztecs, and marched upon Tenochtitlan,

463

The Norman Conquest

When Edward the Confessor died, Harold Godwinson was crowned king of England. William, Duke of Normandy was enraged because he believed Edward wanted him to be the next king. William also said Harold had made a solemn promise to support him. William led an army across the channel and faced Harold at the battle of Hastings, 14 October, 1066. The fight was close, but Harold was eventually killed when an arrow shot by one of William's archers hit him in the eye.

464

William of Normandy wasn't the only ruler interested in becoming king of England. Just before the battle of Hastings, Harold had had to march north to Yorkshire very quickly to fight his brother Tostig and Harald Hardrada, king of Norway. The battle of Stamford Bridge (September, 1066) was a victory for Harold, but instead of being able to rest his men, he had to march them at top speed back down the length of England to fight William!

Turquoise mosaic mask of Quetzalcoatl.

the Aztec capital. The emperor Moctezuma II and his people thought that he was the god Quetzalcoatl and so did not attack him until it was too late. Instead they gave him gifts, including a mask of Quetzalcoatl. Thousands of Aztecs including Moctezuma were killed.

An Aztec poem about the conquest:

Broken spears lie in the roads
we have torn our hair in our grief
the houses are roofless now, and
their walls are red with blood.

462

There were probably about twenty million people living in ancient Mexico in AD 1500, including the Aztecs, Maya and Mixtecs. One hundred years later, there were only about one or two million native people left. Europeans had brought new diseases, war and slavery, with dreadful results.

Writing

Clay tablet with pictograms recording the allocation of beer, around 3100–3000 BC.

465

The oldest written language in the world is probably ancient Sumerian. The oldest inscription dates back to about 3300 BC. The first written signs were pictograms (picture signs). These were gradually simplified and developed into cuneiform script.

A boy's schoolwork is written on this clay tablet in cuneiform script. From around 1900–1700 BC.

466

Ancient Sumerians used a reed stylus (pen) to make wedge-shaped signs. 'Cuneiform' means 'wedge-shaped'. They pressed the stylus into tablets of clay. The clay dried into hard tablets which have survived very well over the centuries. At first Sumerian people kept day to day records, but soon they wrote down dictionaries, stories and even prayers. Many school tablets survive, with daily lessons.

467

The people living in the Indus Valley of India over 4000 years ago developed a writing system based on pictographs, which we still cannot decipher.

Egyptian funeral stela (gravestone) inscription giving the name and titles of Horiraa, an important priest of Ptah at Memphis.

468

The ancient Egyptians developed their hieroglyphic picture-writing more than 5,000 years ago. 'Hieroglyphs' means 'sacred carvings' because the writing usually appeared in sacred places such as monuments and temples. A hieroglyph can stand for a sound, an idea or a whole word. Some hieroglyphic signs are complicated but some are quite simple. The hieroglyph for 'town' is a circle with two roads crossing it.

The hieroglyph for 'town'.

469

Egyptian hieroglyphs can be read either from right to left or left to right. How do you know which way? Look at which direction the animals and birds are facing, and read towards them.

These beautiful coloured hieroglyphs should be read from left to right. They are written on a coffin of the Middle Kingdom period.

141

The Rosetta Stone, carved in 196 BC.

471

Until the Rosetta Stone was discovered in 1799, nobody could read Egyptian hieroglyphs. The Rosetta Stone had the same text on it in three different scripts: hieroglyphs, demotic (everyday Egyptian) and ancient Greek. Scholars used their knowledge of Greek to crack the code.

472

There was a race to crack the Rosetta Stone code. Two scholars, Thomas Young, an English physicist, and the Frenchman Jean-François Champollion, both competed to decipher the Rosetta Stone first. Young worked out that some of the letters made up the sounds of the name of Ptolemy V, but it was Champollion who then realised that the other hieroglyphs made up the sounds of letters and syllables.

470

It's probably the best technological invention ever! The idea of an alphabet was most likely invented in ancient Palestine and Syria around 3,600 years ago. As it was passed across the world, different alphabets developed, such as the Greek alphabet, the Cyrillic alphabet and the Roman alphabet, which is used to write many western languages today.

ABCDEFGHIJKLMNOPQRSTUVWXYZ

473

The Greek alphabet is the ancestor of all modern European alphabets. It was developed around 900 BC from the Phoenician alphabet. It was the first to use vowel sounds as well as consonants, which made it extremely flexible and useful. Classical Greek had 24 letters, the first being alpha, and the last omega.

The ancient Greek alphabet.

Αα alpha	Ηη eta	Νν nu	Ττ tau
Ββ beta	Θθ theta	Ξξ xi	Υυ upsilon
Γγ gamma	Ιι iota	Οο omicron	Φφ phi
Δδ delta	Κκ kappa	Ππ pi	Χχ chi
Εε epsilon	Λλ lamda	Ρρ rho	Ψψ psi
Ζζ zeta	Μμ mu	Σς sigma	Ωω omega

474

Early Greek writing was sometimes known as boustrophedon, or 'ox-turning', because it was written left to right then right to left, like an ox going backwards and forwards ploughing.

475

Romans wrote and spoke Latin, which is one of the roots of today's English language (and many other European languages).

476

Over 3,000 years ago in ancient Crete they used three different writing systems. One of them – called Linear B – was cracked in 1952 by the architect Michael Ventris. He proved that it was based on ancient Greek, a discovery which caused great surprise at the time. Two of the Cretan writing systems, Linear A and a kind of hieroglyphs only found in Crete, are still a mystery.

Part of a tablet showing Linear B writing from Crete. It was written around 1450–1400 BC.

477

The Aztecs compiled sacred books, from which we get our detailed knowledge of their civilization. They used a form of picture-writing which recorded numbers, dates and names, but they had no way of representing sounds or parts of words, so their writing cannot really be called a whole script in the same way as Egyptian hieroglyphs.

478

Most Anglo-Saxons could not read and write. When they did, however, they used letters called runes. Their alphabet was called the futhork (look at the first six letters to see why). The Vikings used a similar kind of alphabet. Runes are designed for carving on to wood, stone or metal, rather than writing with a pen. Sometimes runes were thought to have magic powers.

479

Some Aztec picture signs stand for things, such as 'mountain' or 'house', and some stand for ideas, such as a temple with its roof off which means 'defeat'.

MOUNTAIN

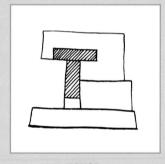

HOUSE

DEFEAT

f	u	th	o	r	k	g	w	h	j	i	n	i	p

x	s	t	b	e	ng	m	l	d	oe	a	ae	y	ea

Anglo-Saxon runes.

480

Chinese was first written down in about 1300 BC. The First Emperor standardized the script between 221 and 210 BC. Certain ancient Chinese characters can still be read easily today. Chinese uses over 50,000 pictograms in all. Luckily you only need to know 3,000 to read a newspaper, but as you can imagine Chinese children spend a lot of time practising their writing.

482

Muslims everywhere learn to read the Qur'an in Arabic script, as this was the language used by Muhammad's followers to write it down originally. The beautiful flowing lines of Arabic script are used to decorate the walls of mosques, as well as many different objects.

481

The art of calligraphy (beautiful writing) has always been held in high esteem in China. The basic tools used by the calligrapher were paper, writing brush, ink and an inkstone, on which the dry ink would be mixed with water. These were known as 'the four treasures of the scholar's studio'.

483

An Arab historian wrote that Muslim scribes had to look after their equipment: 'It is necessary for the scribe to do his utmost to adorn the pen-box, to make it excellent and to look after it.' The owner of this pen-box has decorated it with a verse from the Qur'an.

Pen box from Iraq, AD 1230–50.

484

The Maya developed a sophisticated writing system which has only recently been deciphered. They used over 800 glyphs (picture-signs) which stand for sounds, words or whole ideas.

Maya glyphs on a doorway listing nine generations of rulers, AD 600–800.

147

Writing equipment

485

The ancient Chinese recorded things on scrolls, long lengths of paper which were rolled up for storage.

Part of the Admonitions Scroll from China, 6th–8th century AD.

486

Because the ancient Chinese wrote on paper, some of their old documents have disintegrated and are lost, though others survive on bamboo or carved in stone.

487

Scribes in ancient Egypt wrote on papyrus, a kind of paper made from reeds. They used a brush made from rushes, and chewed the end to separate the fibres. The brush was dipped into water then wiped across a tablet of ink. Writing was mainly in black, with red sometimes used to highlight important words.

488

The first libraries were put together in ancient Sumer around 2700 BC. They contained clay tablets covered in cuneiform writing.

489

The Egyptian hieroglyphic sign for 'writing' was made up from pictures of a scribe's palette and brush case.

490

Early Greek books were long rolls of papyrus. They were rolled up with the end that had the book title on the inside, so it was less likely to be damaged.

493

Ogham is the oldest Celtic writing system known. The Ogham alphabet was used in Ireland from about the fourth century, and sometimes in Cornwall, Scotland and Wales where Irish people settled. Straight lines and notches were carved down the sharp edges of stone or wood. There were twenty letters in Ogham. Only very short inscriptions have been found using Ogham.

491

Aztec and Maya books are called codices. They are made from long strips of fig bark folded like a concertina, with covers made from jaguar skin.

Codex Zouche-Nuttall, Mixtec, AD 1200–1521.

492

There were hundreds of thousands of Aztec and Maya books, made from animal skin or tree-bark paper, but most were destroyed by the Spaniards after they conquered Mexico. The Spaniards thought that books about the Aztec religion were evil.

494

Paper was invented in China in the first century BC.

495

Wax tablets were the most common way of writing in the Roman world. A layer of wax was spread over a flat surface, such as a small piece of wood. Marks could be made on the wax with a sharp stylus (pen) made of metal or bone. When the message was old, the surface could be smoothed to use again.

Wooden base for a Roman wax writing tablet and two styli (pens). 1st or 2nd century AD.

496

To keep their letters private, people in ancient times used a variety of seals. A popular type of seal to keep a letter shut used a blob of melted wax. When it was soft this could be stamped with the owner's special mark.

Seal shaped like a lion's paw with animal head from Anatolia (modern Turkey), 1920–1800 BC.

497

The first books in Britain were religious texts, hand-written in Latin and illustrated by monks, such as the scholars at Lindisfarne monastery in Northumberland, who wrote the Lindisfarne Gospels. There was no paper so they wrote on specially treated animal skins. One very big book used the skins of fifty sheep.

498

Animal skins prepared for writing are usually called 'parchment'. Mostly they are skins of sheep, calves or goats, though sometimes skins of animals such as antelopes or ostriches were used. Vellum is top-grade parchment, made from the skins of very young calves.

499

Mesopotamian clay tablets were sometimes put into clay 'envelopes' before being sent. The envelopes were sealed with cylinder seals. These were small stone cylinders carved with patterns or pictures, which would be rolled along the clay tablet, leaving an impression behind. This letter is from one brother to another, telling of how winter has come and his family have no food, clothes or fuel. It was put into an envelope before being sent.

Clay tablet and its 'envelope' (below). Around 1850 BC.

500

Archaeologists have found Roman documents written in ink on wooden tablets. One wooden tablet was an invitation to a birthday party from one lady to another. It was found at Vindolanda Fort on Hadrian's Wall in northern Britain.

Birthday party invitation.
Around AD 97–103.

Find out more

Of course, there are lots more than 500 things to know about history. If you'd like to discover more, here are some suggestions to get you started.

Books

Mike Corbishley, *The British Museum Illustrated Encyclopaedia of Ancient Rome*, British Museum Press 2003

Carolyn Howitt, *The British Museum Quiz Book of the Ancient World*, British Museum Press 2004

Geraldine Harris and Delia Pemberton, *The British Museum Illustrated Encyclopaedia of Ancient Egypt*, British Museum Press 2005

Sean Sheehan, *The British Museum Illustrated Encyclopaedia of Ancient Greece*, British Museum Press 2002

Katharine Wiltshire, *The British Museum Timeline of the Ancient World*, British Museum Press 2004

Websites

Visit the British Museum website **www.thebritishmuseum.ac.uk** which has lots of information and activities for families and children in the Explore section.

You can also explore these fantastic interactive websites:

www.ancientchina.co.uk
www.earlyimperialchina.co.uk
www.mughalindia.co.uk
www.ancientcivilizations.co.uk
www.ancientegypt.co.uk
www.ancientgreece.co.uk
www.mesopotamia.co.uk
www.ancientindia.co.uk